Be MAGNIFICENT!

Exceed Your Expectations

By Michael Rice

Elements of the Community, Inc

Be Magnificent! Exceed Your Expectations

Published in the United States by Elements of the Community, Inc.

An imprint of the Elements of the Community Publishing Group

ISBN-13: 978-0-578-44832-9

ISBN-10: 0-578-44832-7

Be Magnificent! Exceed Your Expectations is a masterpiece of networking and community empowerment where an individual can implement his strategies in not only accomplishing their individual goals but also improving their community and the systems that impact the lives of others.

David Edmonds, Director,
Philadelphia Department of Human Services

***

This book is magnificent! Awesome, inspiring, motivating and full of nuggets for a person to succeed and leaders to be successful.

Deborah Burnett

Acknowledgements

First and foremost, thank God.

I recognize that there is a Force that sends challenges and obstacles to test to see if I really wanted the things, I said I desired.

Thank you to anyone who has ever said to me, "Good job, I believe in you". "You are special, keep doing what you are doing". Those words help validate, motivate and inspire me to stay on the path in which I was pursuing. The voice of the higher power was speaking through those people and I was grateful for those words of encouragement.

I have to acknowledge my teachers, students, colleagues, coworkers, allies and opponents both on the job and in the street, who help me grow everyday.

It's the inspiration of the community folks, the advocates and activists who inspired and encouraged me to meet the challenges and share in a common mission. My gratitude goes out to the members of EPIC – Equal Partners in Change Community Stakeholder groups and the Philadelphia Youth Leadership Council who patiently and attentively participated in my workshops and acknowledged the impact on their lives and community.

Of course, thanks to my family especially my sisters Paula and Johann for always remaining by my side and having my back. My daughters: Natasha and Mik'ael who represent the legacy. My nieces Mykeeya, Tiffany, Rasheeda, Shonda and my nephew "Little Carl" who continue to exceed expectations.

TABLE OF CONTENTS

Today I am Magnificent!

Today I accept the power I have been blessed with and recognize that to whom much is given, much is expected.

Today I will live with purpose on purpose. I will move forward with intention.

Today I will review my goals and take another step closer to achievement.

Today I will smile at people and recognize my power to make people smile.

Today my "hello's" and "how you doings" will be filled with love and I will make my friends, colleagues, coworkers and acquaintances feel that love.

Today I will recognize the beauty around me and enjoy the abundance in my life.

Today I will use my power to create positive outcomes. Today I move, make decisions and take actions without fear.

Today I will live my life like a Lion aggressively, fiercely and powerfully.

Today I am Magnificent!

Preface

As I write this, the City of Philadelphia celebrates their first Super Bowl victory. This Super Bowl victory was shared by millions of fans who attended the Championship parade on Broad Street and the fantastic crowd outside the Philadelphia Museum of Art. This victory is significant because it comes after years and years of the team struggling to get respect and recognition as a legitimate Super Bowl contender.

The Eagles had a great start to the year by winning 10 games after a less than impressive preceding year. Two years ago, under Coach Chip Kelly, the team was stripped of its key players and devastated by the new coach's plan. This plan almost destroyed the team before he was fired. He traded away the stars of the team believing his coaching scheme was more important than the veteran players that the prior coach had assembled. Initially, they won a few games, but later it became apparent the rest of the league figured out his strategy and quickly adjusted. The results was a losing season, poor morale and a less than enthusiastic fan base.

Two years later, the team appeared to make a comeback. However, 2017 was filled with many hurdles. The team suffered multiple injuries and lost key players including a running back, a defensive end, the kicker and even the newly acquired MVP candidate; wonder boy named Carson Wentz. He went down with a season ending injury while running in a touchdown.

The coach, Doug Pederson was a former Eagles quarterback whose performance as a quarterback was mediocre at best and overshadowed by the upcoming of hope for a future quarterback; Randall Cunningham. Pederson ended up becoming the quarterback coach for the Kansas City Chiefs coached by Andy Reid who was fired by the Eagles several years before. He had no head coaching experience in the NFL. One former coach commented, "he was by far the worse coach in the league".

The Eagles started the season spectacularly, wiping out opponents left and right. The new star quarterback was destined to become the MVP of the league. Then the worst thing that could happen – happened. In the final games of the season, MVP player Quarterback Wentz goes down with ACL injury, which puts him out for the season. The media says, "that's it for the Eagles". The miraculous year for the Eagles is over. Coach Pederson brings in their second-string quarterback off the bench, Nick Foles. Foles, who incidentally was the back up, quarterback for the Chiefs. Foles had one good year with the Eagles but was traded after he failed to perform in subsequent seasons. The rumor was Foles had considered retiring and this was probably his last season. In fact, during the preseason, Foles rarely scrimmaged.

Although the Eagles won the division, thoroughly defeating the Minnesota Vikings, who boasted the best defense in the league, they were still considered the underdogs. They got no respect from the media or other teams.

Then something amazing happened to the Eagles. Although known to choke in the last minute in previous seasons, they adopted the "underdog" title and wore it proudly. Against all the odds, they made it to the Super Bowl. Their final game of the season was against the five-time world champion New England Patriots. The Patriots had a superstar quarterback Tom Brady, who had led the team to numerous championships. It was the classic David vs. Goliath but now Foles vs. Brady.

After an intense, fingernail biting, edge of your seat battle the Eagles prevailed. By combining a relentless attitude, a master game strategy, determination, persistence and raw guts, the Eagles defeated the five-time world champions becoming the winners of the 52nd Super bowl.

Jason Kelce, the Eagles center gave a speech on the Philadelphia Art Museum steps in which recalled the doubters and naysayers who said, "they couldn't make it".

He explained, there was a sign outside the Eagles locker room at the Nova Care center, which stated, "Hungry dogs run faster". Truly, it was the "hunger" to win and the pain of the disrespect they felt that caused the Philadelphia Eagles to run faster, hit harder and play more determined then the former champions.

Such is the premise of this book. The Eagles never gave up even when no one believed in them, they believed in themselves. They did not listen to the naysayers and they played one game at a time. They used strategy, tactics and pure "we expect to win" attitude to execute a winning season. The Eagles played a **magnificent** game on January 2018.

They exceeded all expectations.

This self-help book was written to support the development of **magnificence** in you. The stories, essays, strategies and mindsets contained have a proven track record. Most of them were written, when I was digging down deep and finding a way to overcome the challenges in my own life. This guide reflects, **"As a man thinketh so he is".** Thinking in a manner that allows success to grow in your life. Life is a constant challenge. Life will throw all types of curve balls at you, just when you think you got it mastered. The minute you rest, life will grab you by the throat and try and choke the hell out of you. Life will hit you like it did the Eagles who over the years would get a good lead in the game, only to allow the other team to make a comeback and lose.

Life is a series of let downs, setbacks and monkey wretches. Just when you think you got it made, life will deal you a losing hand. It's the guys that never give up that make it.

In a boxing match, it's not the guy who listens to his corner when they tell him to stay down that becomes the champion. It's the one who acts in spite of the odds. Those who gets up despite the pain and the one that tries again despite what others tell him is the reality. Being **Magnificent** means getting up when everyone counts you out. Being **Magnificent** is having and listening to an inner voice. Being **Magnificent** is recognizing and manifesting your destiny.

Believe me I know what it means when the only faith I had was what I had on the inside. Years before, I lay on a hospital bed with people standing around me crying and thinking it was my last moment. Meanwhile, the sound of a heart monitor was ticking off the seconds of my life; my doctors stood around with doubtful expressions on their faces. I thought to myself many people think they seen my glory, but none know the pain and anguish of my story.

As I lay there connected to ventilator, respirator and heart monitor my thoughts were, "I'm not going out like that". My mind took me back to growing up in the inner city of Philadelphia, where you had to develop an inner toughness to get you through. Our challenges were gang wars, drugs, poverty and violence. In order to make it out, you had to listen to the positive "inner voice."

Manifest Your Destiny

You must decide what you want to do with your life and then do it. Many people talk about success, but few define it for themselves. If you grew up in the inner city, "*survival*" was the first thing you thought about, success was a dream.

First, define what success means to you. Many people embark upon a journey with no destination and when they do reach the end of the trail, they feel unfulfilled because they never set perimeters for their own personal success. **"Success is a journey"**. The perquisite is to smell the flowers along the way. Celebrating the little victories lead to bigger victories. You got to give yourself credit for trying because you know the path to victory is paved with failures. **Magnificent people** realize that failures are lessons. Even if you lose, don't lose the lesson, which means if you learn something, you win.

Many people are concerned with whose watching. They listen to the negative comments, become self-conscious and lose their focus. **Focus is Follow one course until success.** Listening to the negativity of others will cause you to lose focus. Listen to the positive inner voice. The voice that encourages, "get up and keep it moving".

Life is a struggle. Frederick Douglas said, "Where there is no struggle there is not progress". Douglas knew he needed to put the work in to reap the benefits of the labor.

"Those who profess to favor freedom and yet depreciate agitation are men who want crops without plowing up the ground. They want rain without thunder and lightning. They want the ocean without the awful roar of its many waters. This struggle may be a moral one; or it may be a physical one; or it may both moral and physical, but it must be a struggle. Power concedes nothing with demand, it never has and never will."

Frederick Douglas

One of my mentors, J. Morris Anderson, founder of the Miss Black America Pageant and former stockbroker turned Producer/activist. He faced many challenges when he took up the fight for Black women because the main stream Miss America Pageant would not recognize the beauty, talent and poise of the African American female. Anderson was inspired because he had beautiful and talented daughters, but he knew they would never become Miss America. He challenged the system and started his own pageant. His pageant gave opportunity to Black women including starts like Oprah Winfrey, Bernadette Stanis and Toni Braxton. Anderson's philosophy was programmed into my mind, **"Sow the seeds of positivity and reap the flowers of success".**

This book is about sowing positive actions and reaping the harvest of your efforts. It's describes **magnificence** and how it is manifested on the world stage and in the inner city. The chapters tell about ordinary individuals recognizing their greatness and allowing it to radiate upon society. There are many extraordinary people who are living ordinary lives and many ordinary people doing extraordinary things.

Whether you are struggling high school student with hopes of going to college, or a corporate professional seeking that next promotion, a concerned block captain charged with organizing the block or an overwhelmed parent trying to make ends meet and keep children safe and aspiring. This book is for you!

Introduction

Are you ready to challenge yourself to take it to the next level? Ready to recognize the greatness you have inside? Ready to acknowledge that you are born with unlimited potential? This book is about challenging yourself to take it to the next level. It's about recognizing and releasing the greatness you have inside. It about knowing that you are born with unlimited potential and that taking action is the next logical step.

Contained within this book are a collection of essays, and stories from my life and the people who surrounded me. Real people, whether they were family, friends, opponents or bullies, who taught me valuable lessons. I share stories about people from Philadelphia, Pa. One reason is because if any of my students or workshop participants read this book, they will know it's the truth. The other reason is that the city is filled with individuals who take on challenges everyday and overcome them.

The lessons can serve as a guide to individuals seeking to perform at the ultimate level.

"Be Magnificent! Exceed Your Expectations" the title of this book suggests two unique yet related concepts of achievement. The first, **"Be Magnificent"** is a demand to pursue excellence in your life. Average is for **"Sheeple"** they are typical people who like the sheep just follow the herd. They follow the crowd instead of becoming the shepherd determining the path and encouraging, prodding and persuading the masses.

The second concept **"Exceed Your Expectations."** Many people expectations of them-selves are low. "People who fail at life, not because they aim too high and miss, but because they aim too low and hit" stated Les Brown. They have low expectations of themselves and live below their potential. They rarely challenge themselves to tap into their true potential. **"Exceed Your Expectations"** infers whatever your goals are, take them one step further. Run the extra lap. Walk the extra mile. Add ten more pounds to your set. Go for the next higher degree. Don't settle just for the GED-go to college. Challenge the impossible.

What Type are You?

There are three types of people. People who make things happen. People who watch things happen and the individuals who wonder what happened. The fact you are reading this book suggests that you are ready to make things happen. Reading books, stories or watching inspirational videos are great tools to motivate, however taking the steps necessary to move yourself forward are essential to exceeding your expectations. Either you are implementing your plan, or you are a part of someone else's plan. You either deploy yourself or you are employed by others.

This book is for people who refuse to become a victim of their circumstance and recognize deep inside they can create constructive change in their lives.

CHILDHOOD

It's report card time in the Rice household. My parents sit on the couch in the living room while my two sisters and I sit in the kitchen waiting our turn to present our report cards. My father was a proud black man who grew up on the streets of North Philly. He grew up hard and worked three jobs most of his life. I was the middle child at the time. Carl and Terry my brothers, were 10 years older and had already moved out on their own. My oldest sister Paula was about 16 years old and my youngest sister Johann was about 8 years old.

It was like a game show waiting in the kitchen for the prompt from our parents. You are the next contestant in the report card game. If you win it may mean money and prizes but if you lose, it could mean a butt whipping and punishment. My sister, Paula was always on the honor roll and a straight "A" student. She had all A's and one B. When she showed her report card to my father, he reviewed it very critically and complained, "What's with the "B"? My sister immediately burst into tears and ran out of the room. I was up next and, in my head, I heard "Michael Rice come on down". This reporting period, I managed to pass all my subjects and was proud to claim all C's on my report card. However, after my sister's performance, I was a little reluctant as I approached my father.

I handed him the report card. He reviewed it with a look of what only could be described as disgust. "What's this?" he barked. I replied, a "C". What's a "C?" he snorted. I proudly replied, "It's average." He came back with some words, I will never forget. They will forever be embedded in my mind. "So, what you want to be? Mediocre!"

Truth be told, I didn't know what "mediocre" meant. I knew by the tone of my father's voice "mediocre" was something I never wanted to become. My immediate thought was at least I'm not failing. According to my father that was not good enough. He emphasized that average was as close to the bottom as it was to the top. Average was nothing. You will not accomplish anything being average. Average is just showing up. It's like being in the Olympics and not placing in the top three; bronze, silver and gold. Sure, you made it to the Olympics, but no one remembers "the also ran".

My father taught me that you stop being average the day you decide to step up, because the average person won't make that decision. Later I would learn that *average people have wishes and hopes. Great people have goals and plans.* This scene played out in my psyche for years. I felt in my heart to become like everyone else was basically expecting less of myself.

You see my father's philosophy was *"no one rises to low expectations."* Although he dropped out of high school, he joined the Army and served in the World War II. After being discharged, he worked three jobs including a full-time job at the Post office. Before he died, he retired and amassed a fortune in real estate and stocks.

He was one of the reasons; I decided not to be mediocre but different. I don't mean different like tattooing my body or wearing outlandish hairdos, but my father taught me to associate pain with being average. Many times, when I got into trouble as a youth, I was following the crowd. He would say with an angry glare, "Are you a follower?" "Follower" became another bad word in my vocabulary.

Although my parents split up early in my adolescence, my father's visits and words were powerful in my life. His legacy lives on. The desire to succeed, led me to become his first child to graduate from college. The legacy did not stop there with my daughter and my sisters' children obtaining colleges degrees as well.

When I graduated from high school, I was the only one among the so called, "boys in the hood" who walked down the aisle to receive my diploma on time. There were many distractions for us growing up in the inner-city including gang warring, drinking wine, smoking weed, chasing girls and running from the police. My friends were equally surprised when I graduated, and they didn't. They remembered the many times, I ditched school to hang with them, but they didn't notice the many times, I ditched them to go to school.

My father was the reason why I was always striving to become different like going into the Navy while my friends joined the Army and National Guard. I now understand my mother's attempts to keep me safe by occupying my time, putting me in special programs and sending me to camp in Poconos every summer. These programs and the mentors who were apart of them, led me to "walk a path less traveled."

My mother taught me to respect women but to create your own standards as a man and live by them. Although she only stood about 5 feet tall when she spoke it was the voice of a giant. She grew up in North Philly with a napoleon complex because she was short and petite with five brothers and four sisters. I'm sure she had to assert her authority many times because of her stature.

She raised three young black boys and two black girls into adulthood. This was major because in my community many of my schoolmates died either from drugs or were murdered by the neighborhood gangs. My mother was a strong and willful woman. She allowed me to grow and assert my independence while putting up with my ignorance and rebellion. She taught me the value of the knowledge found in books. Our living room had bookcases filled with books. My mother sat in her favorite chair, reading glasses on her nose, cigarette in one hand and book in another. Although, she only had a high school diploma, she would brag she had a college education on her bookshelf. My father would give me books as a gift. I treasured them. This upbringing caused an irresistible urge to read and learn about new things and new ideas.

My siblings and I grew up on the mean streets of Philadelphia at a time when gang warfare was at an all time high. There were over six hundred gangs throughout the city. Every day following the school day, there will daily gang wars right outside our homes. It was not unusual to see someone stabbed or shot outside your door. If you were not a member of a gang, you were harassed daily for money and sometimes for your sneakers or shoes. Everyday there were thugs waiting outside the entrances at school to rob you of change. A common response to the daily shake down, "I don't have any money" and the thugs would reply, "All I find I can have," while patting your pockets for anything of value.

Racial tensions were also hot and heavy during these years. I was bussed from an all-black Cleveland Elementary School in North Philadelphia to an all-white Olney Elementary school in the segregated Northeast Philadelphia. Sometimes the white kids from the nearby High School would come by and call us names and spit on us. We knew nothing of racism then, but we sure learned fast.

In the classrooms in Wagner Junior High, I witnessed gangs of young boys, beating and stomping classmates. This is probably where my loyalty grew for the underdog.

Since my siblings were so much older than me, by the time I reached adolescence, they were out the household leaving my youngest sister and me. My parents taught me to protect my younger sister at all costs. I fought many battles with individuals who were bigger and stronger than me, because they were messing with my little sister. It was then I learned sometimes you got to fight even when "it's not about you." I learned when fighting for a **cause**, you will find courage and strength you did not know you had.

Better than Average

During my life's journey, I concluded that if you strive to become average and you don't measure up, you end up being less than average which puts you somewhere very close to failing. Think about it. If you strive to be great and you fall short you still end up way ahead of the average person.

To be **"Magnificent"** means to be greater than you were. Being Magnificent is the state of magnifying your efforts and your outcomes. When you are learning and developing yourself, you are becoming magnificent. The ending result is Magnificence. I heard, if you reach for the stars, and you get the clouds, you still have accomplished a lot. If you set your goal to become magnificent and you end up excellent, you have added significant value to yourself and made a significant impact on the world.

There is a big difference in your attitude whether you are just trying to pass a test in school or if you are striving for an "A". Going for the "A" takes courage; just trying to pass the test is based in fear and laziness.

Going to the gym one day, Motoe a tough gang member called me out. He wanted to slap box with me. He had his partners around him and I guess he thought it would be fun. Now I was somewhat of a nerd at the time. While Motoe spent his time, running wild in the street. I spend my time reading comic books and racing my HO cars.

Once we started boxing, I realized that I was faster than Motoe and hit harder. He was bobbing and weaving but I could hit him at will. He remarked to his friends that I had a "heavy hand". I imagined that I could win this boxing match. But I realized if I beat Motoe he would become embarrassed. It also meant I could end up boxing the rest of the gang. I knew they would want to test me out.

LOSING WAS MY COMFORT ZONE.

Instead of living out my potential, I played average. Fear of success filled my mind. Funny, I was not worried about losing. Losing meant the status quo remained and I was safe. Losing was my comfort zone

Fear of Success

In school, it was just like that. If you asked too many questions in class like you really wanted to learn something, you may be ostracized. If you answered too many questions asked by the teacher, you could be labeled a geek. This was dangerous because it made you a target for the bullies. Being smart was not cool. A lot of these youth had taken this behavior into adulthood. They never really lived their true potential because they were afraid that it would not look cool. Soon their ignorance became a reality.

Many people live their lives this way and never reach their fullest potential because they are afraid of the challenge of living on the next level. The next level is outside your comfort zone. The next level is growth. Most of us, don't strive to be great because we fear the feeling of being inadequate if we fail. We are afraid of the obstacles and challenges that come with success. We fear success.

What we really need to focus on is the ecstasy of success. Pursuing success can become addictive, and when you are successful the feeling is intoxicating. One of the greatest feelings is to overcoming obstacles in order to get what is deserved. We value things more when we work for it. There's a big difference between running in a race and winning a trophy, then someone giving you a trophy just because you showed up. One represents your ability, determination and commitment, while the other has little value or meaning. When you learn to welcome adversity as your friend. Adversity is going to help you grow and turn challenges into opportunities. Life is different and can become a promise. A promise you are determined to fulfill.

One of the lessons in this book came to me during a training seminar with about 25 participants. As part of an icebreaker exercise, each participant talked about a challenge they were facing in their lives. By the end of the exercise, everyone in the room spoke about major obstacles they were dealing with while trying to complete the yearlong training. These challenges were not little distractions. They talked about family members dying, dealing house fires, losing all their possessions, losing their homes, taking care of senior family members, dealing with challenges from their children, overcoming physical and mental obstacles, fighting addiction, financial issues and more. Even with all these challenges, they stuck to it and completed the yearlong training.

Each one of these individuals desired to be better than they were. They sought excellence in their lives. They weren't satisfied with where they were in their life. They consciously decided that in spite major obstacles to become better.

Who should read this book?

This book was written for the class of trainees who despite their challenges, choose to reach for the stars. It was written for the youth leader who has decided they don't want to be mediocre and that they have something special to offer the world. It's for the angry and frustrated community person who's tired of his community being overlooked and neglected. It's for the downtrodden individual who is frustrated with being depressed, poor and broken. I wrote this book for those who are disgusted with living a "half behind life". It was written for anyone who has decided that instead of being a pretender and faking the game, they wanted to be a contender and win the game.

This book is dedicated to the person who has decided that every setback in their life was there so they could come back stronger than ever. It's for all those so-called ordinary people who know in their hearts that they are extraordinary. I started to call this book, "**Things I wish my father had told me.**" This is because a lot of the tips here are advice coming from the heart of someone who cares about your outcomes in life while acknowledging that you need discipline along with love.

People say, "If I had known back then what I know now, I would be so much farther along in life". They believe knowing these little tidbits early in life would have made things a lot easier. Many books tell you what to do; however, few tell you what you need to think about and how to control your thinking. The contents of this book are fundamental principles explained so anyone can understand and utilize them in their lives.

***

Today you realized you always had the power. Now you are ready to harness and unleash the Beast within. The beast is that drive to win, that irresistible urge, the unrelenting confidence, that driving force that wakes you up everyday and lets you know your desires are about to be obtained. **Becoming Magnificent** is about living your life to the fullest potential. **Becoming Magnificent** is about reaching beyond your expectations. It about being all you can become and more. It's a book about exceeding and excelling.

Exceed your Expectations
Be better
Be Excellent
Be Magnificent!

Chapter One

VISION

"Where there is no vision, there is no hope"

George Washington Carver

Your ability to see the future, as you would like it to become will directly correlate with your ability to make it happen. If you can't visualize it you will not be able to create it.

The "vision" is not about seeing what is directly in front of you. It's about seeing your "desired future". It's about creating in your head a "future reality. Through consistent action you will bring out the "future reality". Vision is the ability to see the future as you desire. All things in life begin with someone having a vision. Amazing things happen when someone takes the invisible (a thought) and makes it visible (a creation).

Every person who has ever done anything significant in his or her life or in the world has started with a "Vision".

During times of oppression and discrimination in Philadelphia, there were leaders who provided vision for the people. Rev. Leon Sullivan was a Baptist preacher from North Philadelphia. When most black folks in

Philadelphia were either unemployed or underemployed, Rev Sullivan had a vision. Although there were dozens of factories with jobs available in the city, if you were black it was nearly impossible to get a job because of segregation laws.

Despite the law, Rev. Sullivan saw a city were black folks worked alongside white people. He saw a city where black people owned property, ran businesses and were treated with dignity and respect. It was because of this vision Rev Sullivan was able to lead hundreds of other black preachers to get their congregations to boycott the products these factories produced. Pretty soon, the companies were knocking on Sullivan's door with jobs. However, he found that many of the people seeking jobs still could not get hired because they lacked the skills. Rev Sullivan built upon this vision and created Opportunities Industrialization Center (OIC), an organization that provide vocational job training.

Nelson Mandela provided a vision for South African people that led them out of the dreadful apartheid.

Gandhi provided a vision for his people who were being oppressed by the British in India.

Martin Luther King, Jr. spoke of a dream for his people during the American civil rights movement.

You as an individual must have your own vision for yourself and your family. In order to create a better reality for yourself, you must see something better in the future.

"The only thing worse than being blind was having sight with no vision,"

Helen Keller.

Many people's vision materializes out of pain.

Robert Hall, founder of Amongst Men, was a foster child who did know his father and his mother abandoned him. Out of his pain, he created a mentoring organization that is in the Philadelphia schools. His vision helped hundreds of youth restore their self-esteem.

Dorothy Speight- Johnson lost her son to gun violence. Out of her pain, she created "Mother's in Charge" to provide comfort and support to families who lost loved ones to violence.

Malik Aziz, Ray Jones, Bilal Quayyum and Mark Harrell, founded "Men United for a Better Philadelphia" because they became tired of seeing young black men gunned down in the streets. Together they had a vision for a better quality of life for young African American males in the city.

Sylvia Simms, school bus matron, got tired of seeing school closings and youth suffering because of it. She had a vision and created "Parent Power", a parent advocacy organization.

Arychie Leacock, founder of the "IDAAY", Institute for the Development of African American Youth, created an initiative focusing on helping youth in the community called, "Don't Fall Down In the Hood."

Kenyatta Johnson found himself facing a gun charge at the age of 16. Turned himself around and created a new future as Councilman over the district where he roamed the streets.

Everywhere there are people with vision who are creating their own reality. **Will Smith,** aka Fresh Prince came from the streets of West Philadelphia and created vision for himself that sent him to Hollywood to become one of the highest paid actors in movies. Smith had vision and created his own reality.

All these individuals wanted something better for themselves and others. They added value to their environment. When you create a vision, make sure in your mind you can see, feel, taste, smell and experience it. Make it real. The more real it is to you the better you can bring it into reality.

When Martin Luther King, Jr. penned the "I have a dream" speech, he spoke of his vision. He presented a clear reality of what he projected for the future.

The amazing thing about having a vision is when clearly expressed, you can get others to share it and help you reach your vision. The only way you can get to what you want in life is to see yourself in it. This is called vision.

The goal is not to live forever, however the goal is create something that will.

"Vision that goes beyond the present but actually brings the future into present reality. Some people see things as they are and say why I dream of things that never were and say, Why not".

George Bernard Shaw

People who have great vision are like the best quarterbacks. Their offense is about being able to see the goal so they can throw a touchdown. It is also about seeing the defense and identifying the obstacles and overcoming them. Successful organizations have "vision statements" that provides a common future that all employees/ supporters of an organization can believe in. Vision statements are essential to strategic plans because they provide a common direction for the company.

Magnificent people take the invisible (thought) and make it visible (reality). When they look into the mirror, they don't see a reflection, they see a projection of what they desire.

Chapter Two

The Three Ps

Purpose, Potential & Passion

━━

"God and Nature first made us what we are, and then out of our own created genius we make ourselves what we want to be. Follow always that great law. Let the sky and God be our limit and Eternity our measurement"

Marcus Garvey

Purpose

Have you ever wondered why you were placed where you are today? Ever question why you have these certain set of friends, family and coworkers around you? Do you think it's an accident you are in this situation; dealing with these circumstances?

Once you realize you are here for a purpose, you will begin to understand your life. Suddenly, you will see there are no coincidences. You will recognize the messages being delivered to you each day. Direction on where your life should go will come to you in the form of insights delivered by friends, colleagues and even strangers. Recognizing your purpose opens your eyes. It gives your life precision, direction and inspiration. It allows you to deal with obstructions, obstacles and challenges with faith, courage and commitment. Purpose allows you to realize what is possible in your life. Purpose gives you expectation. Knowing your purpose will allow you to rise above your present circumstance. It will give you a powerful sense of confidence, that there is more to your life then you are presently experiencing. It will move you beyond where others say "what if" or "yeah but" when it comes to tapping your true potential. You will stop seeing obstacles because your eyes will only see your goals.

Understanding your purpose will let you see that you were "built for your goals". You were placed on the earth for a reason and given everything you need in order to accomplish it. You are like a car built for a given purpose. Your skills are like the V8 engine that makes you go and those wheels that make it easy to move.

You are like a bird given wings because you were meant to fly. Your skills, the tools and the abilities are inherent. But like that bird you got to spread your wings. No one can do that for you. Like a car, you got to turn the key and step on the gas. It's up to you.

Open your eyes and ears to the messages surrounding you. The clues about what to do to fulfill your purpose are around you. They are in the supermarket, on the job and at the mall. They are in everything that you do and everywhere that you go.

Focus on your purpose and how they will occur will happen right before your eyes. Call it the law of attraction or destiny. It's like that movie "Field of Dreams" where Kevin Costner says, "Build it and they will come". Accept your purpose and the way to get there will appear. With knowledge of purpose attracts your vehicle for arrival. Faith is the belief in unseen and certainty of the unknown. Faith and purpose walk hand in hand.

Potential

The best way to explain "potential" is to think of a baby learning to walk. You can model the behavior and you can hold their hand but eventually a baby walks on their own. A baby is born with the ability to walk. Your potential is your capacity to develop ability and to become something in the future. Just like a baby has potential to walk when it is born, you have the abilities and skills that should be developed for you to reach your potential.

Potential is the connection between vision and purpose. Your vision is your potential, visually realized in your mind. While your purpose gives your direction, your potential gives you a glimpse of just how far you can go.

Indications of your potential reveal themselves at an early age. Therefore is vitally important to expose yourself to as many faucets of life as possible. Think of realizing your potential as picking up a pen and drawing a picture. Some people are born with gifts of art and music. However, they never realize them because they never pick up a paintbrush, an instrument or a microphone. Your potential has no limits once you realize the power you possess. Now I'm not saying you can do or be anything. Everyone is not born to be a doctor or lawyer, scientist or astronaut. However, when you discover your purpose you now have a roadmap to fulfilling your potential.

Muhammad Ali was destined to become a three-time heavyweight champion. He changed the sport of boxing. Yet, Muhammad Ali probably would have made a lousy doctor or astronaut. When he discovered his purpose to become a great boxer, he was able to fulfill his potential.

Rev. Myles Monroe defined potential by comparing it to an apple seed. He asked, "what is the potential of an apple?" You may respond the potential of an apple is to produce an apple tree. However, if you think further you realize in every apple, there is the potential to create hundreds of trees and even orchards. The potential of an apple seed is limitless. Yet an apple seed cannot produce an orange tree or a peach tree. It's the same as identifying your purpose. You will discover where your potential lies.

Passion

Passion is the fuel feeding your purpose and moves you to tap into your potential. Passion is a feeling of intense enthusiasm and compelling desire for something or someone. Your purpose is often revealed by your passion. It's hidden inside you like the prize inside the crackerjack box. Your passion is often a talent that comes easy. Talent is a natural, innate skill. Always work your talent until you become good at it because hustle beats talent on any given day. Talent is a head start for what is to come for you. When you enjoy doing something, and you repeatedly do it and then you become skilled. Skill is talent refined. A person enjoys working on cars often becomes a skilled mechanic. A child who enjoys music often becomes a skilled vocalist or musician.

Your passion is energy. It gives you strength and power to move and accomplish. It is an endless flow of fuel toward your purpose and goals in life. The passion you feel can be seen and felt by others. It cannot only motivate you but acts as a flame to ignite passion in others. Passion can become like electricity, invisible yet powerful.

Purpose, potential and passion used together makes you unstoppable in reaching your goals. Post your purpose and major goals where you can see them. Use your mirrors, refrigerators and walls as a beacon to remind you of your reason for living. Use meditation in the morning and evening to energize your passion. Focus on fulfilling your potential. Connect it to your vision. As you meditate, reinforce that it is your destiny and see yourself moving closer and closer towards its manifestation everyday.

BONUS FOR READERS – Wow, you are up to chapter three already. Feel free to keep notes and write in the margins. Want to keep current with the latest ideas, tips and advice on how you can be the best you can? Visit www.michaelricespeaks.com and sign up. You also can email me at theConnector@verizon.net if you have any questions.

Chapter Three

You are what you think!

"As a man thinketh in his heart so is he".

James Allen

You are what you think. Powerful yet simple words; think and become. Your thoughts become action. Consistent action develops a habit. Your habits reveal your character and your character determines your destiny.

Victor Frankl, the author of **Man's Search for Meaning** said, "Man does not simply exist but always decides what his existence will be, what he will become in the next moment".

Who you are and what you are is dependent on what you think about yourself? Change happens when you control your thoughts and act upon them consistently with a definite purpose in mind.

Herbert Harris, author of "**The Universal Laws of Success,**" states "How you see yourself in your own eyes determines what you get out of life. Self-image is your own conception of yourself. It is the mental and emotional picture you hold in your own consciousness of who you are, what you are and what you represent."

If you want to change yourself image, you must change the conversation you have with yourself everyday. Your self-image is based upon what other's think of your actions as you develop. The self-image comes from the input you received from childhood. It is based upon the opinion of people whose judgment you value. You adopt other's input as your own self-talk reaffirming positive or negative images of yourself.

Dr. John Churchville is an unsung hero in the Philadelphia civil rights movement. He is one of the founders of the Freedom School, a defense attorney, a teacher, and a radio personality. He revealed in one of his leadership seminars that his grandmother had a great influence on him. He stated that she constantly told him that he was lazy, shiftless and would never amount to anything. She insisted that he would become an alcoholic like his father. Churchville disclosed that he fought with the voice of his grandmother for years inside his head. He stated she said it so much that eventually he began telling himself that he was lazy and no good. For years, Churchville would fight with the fear of becoming an alcoholic like his father.

My youngest daughter, **Mika'el** was always the teacher's pet in elementary school. However, when she transferred to middle school, she did not do well on her first reporting period. She had always been self-motivated. I think she really enjoyed the positive attention she received when she did well in school. When I sat down to talk to her, I told her that I was not upset. I explained to her that we are a family of smart people. Everyone in the family is smart. Therefore, I know she had the potential to do better. I let her know if she needed some help to let me know but I was not going to discipline her or yell and scream. Sure enough, the next reporting period her grades improved. I share this story because years later, we were walking down the street and she remarked to me, Dad, "I'm smart and I think I get that from you." I smiled because this seed was planted years before. My conversation with her became her own self-talk. Her self-talk lead her to get her degree from Drexel University.

Your mother's words impact you today. If she told you that you were sloppy and unorganized, you may adopt a sloppy and chaotic lifestyle. You believe deep in your heart that you are a sloppy person. You believe this even though outwardly you deny it. You still hear your mother's voice inside your head.

Your belief binds you to certain behaviors. You cannot change until you change your belief. You cannot change your belief until you change your self-talk about yourself.

How do you change your self-talk that is programmed in her head? The answer is changing your programming. Your mind is like a computer. A computer is actually useless without the software or programming.

Once you input the programming you desire, a computer will perform the tasks you request. Your mind is no different. It needs the appropriate programming in order to meet your needs.

In the case of your mind, the software is affirmations. Affirmations are statements of fact in the future. An affirmation is a positive statement of your desired self-image. Affirmations can be used to change behaviors and to maintain an improved self-image. For example, your affirmation to counteract your mother's programming would be,

> "I am a neat and organized person. I always keep my home organized, neat and clean."

You would say this to yourself in the morning when you wake up and, in the evening, before you retire. Now combine this practice with visualization. Visualization is using your imagination to create a vivid picture of the self-image you desire or the goals you wish to achieve. Your brain cannot distinguish between something you vividly imagine and something you experience. Picture your home neat and clean. See yourself actively cleaning and organizing your space. Imagine your house or apartment as organized, orderly and well kept.

Now say with passion:

"I am a neat and well-organized person. I always keep my home clean, neat and organized. Everyday I am becoming more and more organized and efficient."

Saying this statement passionately to your-self with emotion is the key. Passion is the spark that energizes your affirmations.

Anthony Robbins, author of **Awaken the Giant Within** states, "If you rehearse the new, empowering alternative again and again with tremendous emotional intensity, you'll carve out a pathway, and with even more repetition and emotion, it will become a highway to this new way of achieving results, and it will become a part of your habitual behavior."

By combining visualization and affirmation in a daily meditation you will create amazing results. The habit of imagining a new pattern of behavior will gradually create a self- image. The power of your mind is infinite. You have the power to obtain your desire and create the world you wish to live in. Take control of your thoughts and you take control of your destiny. Thoughts, focused upon, become action.

However, just thinking about getting your home or office organized is not enough. You must act on your thoughts. Your affirmations will help motivate you to action. Plan your actions in a systematic and strategic manner. Consistency in your actions is the secret ingredient. You must consistently act on your thoughts on a regular basis. While affirmations will help you move forward, it's the action that counts. Thinking and talking will not change your life but acting will. Your actions must be consistent on a regular basis. You must train yourself by creating daily rituals, which reinforce your thoughts and your goals. Everyday when you perform the action think to yourself, I am getting closer and closer to my desired goal. In addition, you should train your mind. Study books and watch videos on the topics and subjects you want to become effective. Embellish yourself into the subject so that you not only desire to become better but know strategies and techniques to perform at a higher level.

How to become more social person

Do you want to become a more outgoing and social individual? You noticed in the past, you have not been invited to parties or special events. On the job, you are not selected for various committees. The colleagues at work did not invite you for happy hour after work or to that after-work event everyone seems to be attending. Are you overlooked at social events and affairs?

Maybe you were not hugged enough as a child. Perhaps you had a traumatic experience with the opposite sex.   Growing up maybe you were physically awkward and were not chosen for the childhood games like basketball, football, baseball or extra curricular activities.   This may have caused you to do more stuff by yourself like read books, collect stamps, coins, play with animals, etc.   All in all, your social self was not developed.

It does not matter.   Forget the past.   Today you have decided to change your relationships by creating change in yourself.   You feel that by improving your relationships with co-workers, friends and colleagues, you will open the door to opportunities.

Develop a Social Habit

The key here is developing a social habit, a consistent pattern of relationship by building behavior. After all, if your goal is to lose weight, you are not going to meet your goal if you exercise sporadically.   If you only exercise when you feel like it or when it's convenient, your goals will never be met.

Become consistent in your outward social behavior.   The added benefit here is by you being consistent in your outgoing behavior; your character will gradually develop you as a friendlier and more outgoing individual.   People will view you as fun, socially able and caring.   They will enjoy having you around.   Soon you will be invited to attend social events and participate in new activities, meetings and committees. People will perceive you as a successful and popular individual. They will see you as an aspiring networker.

Here is a three-step process for creating a more social self. You must practice this process daily at least twice a day. However, after about 20 days of practice, it will become natural for you. The process will sink into your subconscious and you and your associates will notice a change in you.

The Steps are

1. Imagination - Assimilation
2. Cut and Paste
3. Affirmation

Step One – Imagination /Assimilation

Close your eyes. Think of an individual whom you admire; someone who exemplifies the qualities of social poise, tact and grace. Look at how they stand and talk. Notice the rhythm of their words, the proximity of space between them. Notice the phases they use and how they touch and engage people as they speak. What are the unique qualities that they possess? It could be their smooth demeanor or the way they walk or the rhythm of their speech. It maybe how they dress and smile.

Open your eyes and write down these qualities. Which qualities do you admire? The qualities you admire are the ones you wish to possess.

Now think of an actor you enjoy. Think of someone who represents cool confidence maybe a character like Idris Elba, Barak Obama, or Denzel Washington or actresses like Angela Bassett, Taraji P Henson or Lupita Nyong'o.

Close your eyes again. Now notice how they move and talk. See yourself standing behind them. Now step into their body; become them. Assimilate their being into yours. Now practice moving and talking like the person you admire. See yourself moving with confidence and poise.

Remember anything that was created in the world started as thought and later through action became reality.

Now exercise two - Cut & Paste

Stop what you are doing and do this one. Close your eyes. Imagine a time when you felt confident and powerful. This may have been after you made an excellent speech or just received an award. It could be the day of your graduation or perhaps, the time when you were able to get the phone number of a person you admired. Maybe you hit a homerun or made a touchdown. You could have just bought a new car or got that promotion.

Capture that ultimate feeling of confidence and well-being. Feel it inside. Breathe the way you would breathe if you were feeling totally confident. Feel your shoulders going back and your chest sticking out. Your head held high and a smile on your face. You feel great.

Now imagine a challenge ahead of you. Maybe you are asking for raise or date or a job. Feel and see yourself with confidence and energy getting the job, making the date and receiving the raise. Picture it in your mind vividly like it's happening now with the energy of the moment.

Okay, open your eyes. Feel good, don't you?

In order to energize your new self-image, you will visualize your new self-interacting with others with poise and confidence. Imagine the conversation, hearing yourself speaking with confidence and see yourself interacting with new people who are smiling and enjoying your company. Feel the confidence growing inside you. This exercise is great for whenever you feel depressed, frustrated or discouraged.

You can alter your emotional state. Control your moods and emotions. Like word processing software, you can take positive moods from the past and cut and paste in the present. You can install whatever emotional state you desire such as confidence, courage, peace of mind etc. Use this exercise whenever you need energy and power for a situation. Fire up your brain with power.

This last exercise will reaffirm your new self. Perform this exercise everyday, twice a day in the morning and in the evening before you retire.

Step Three – Verbal Affirmation

In order to establish yourself as a successful social individual, you will need to download the software of an individual who possesses the qualities of Savoir-Faire. Savoir-Faire is a quality or skill of a social individual. Savoir-Faire is French phrase, which means to know what to do, what to say and how to act in any given situation. A person who is considered Savoir-faire possesses the qualities of social poise, grace and confidence.

You will download those qualities by using above steps and using the Verbal Affirmation method. While you can develop your own affirmation, start with this example first.

Your verbal affirmation would sound like this:

I have now discovered the latent power of Savoir-Faire in my mind.

I am attractive, outgoing and confident.

Everyday I am attracting new people into my life.

I always begin each conversation with a complement.

I am charming and articulate.

I love meeting new people.

I am always dress appropriately for every occasion.

I am always positive and courteous in my conversations.

I listen carefully and strategically.

I am confident, attractive and outgoing.

People love me.

The more I love myself the more love I have to give to others.

I am appropriate, timely and correct.

I am a powerful individual.

I am Savoir-Faire.

Memorize this affirmation and use it as a power tool for your self-confidence and social self. The more you use it, the more powerful it will become in your life.

Don't forget to study books and watch YouTube videos on affirming your confident self. The more techniques you learn, the more tools you will have in your toolbox.

You have the power!

Remember, it started as a thought that you actualized into an action. You make the action consistent and it becomes a habit. Habitually executing this action, it becomes part of your character. Your character determines your destiny, but it all starts with the thought process.

James Allen, author of the book, **"As a Man thinketh"** points out that a man's character is the complete sum of all his thoughts.

You decide what you will become and who you will be at any given moment. The world you live in is decided by you, those thoughts start in your mind. If you decide you are a success, then you are. If you decide you are a failure, then you are. You create your own reality.

Using empowering exercises, you can change habits, character and destiny.

"Remember, you are what you think."

Be Magnificent! Exceed Your Expectations

Chapter Four

Meeting the Challenge

"The ultimate measure of a man is not where he stands during moments of comfort and convenience, but where he stands during times of challenge and controversy."

Dr. Martin Luther King, Jr.

Everyone has challenges in their lives. EVERYONE! Some people don't display the challenges in their lives. Some people wear it like a badge of honor. It's not a question whether or not life will challenge you, it's a question of when and are you prepared. What is your Mindset?

"Life is not all sunshine and rainbows. It can be a mean and nasty place and I don't care how tough you are, it will beat you to your knees and keep you there permanently if you let it. You, me or nobody is gonna hit as hard as life. But it ain't about how hard ya hit, it about how hard you can get hit and keep moving forward. It's about how hard you can take a hit and keep moving forward. That's how winning is done."

Rocky Balboa

That's success! The real winners can take a punch and shake it off. Life will test you to see if you are serious about what you want. Many people give up with the first sign of resistance. They are the pretenders, they pretend they want to reach a goal but really, they are not willing to do what is necessary in order to obtain it. Pretenders wish for things. Contenders expect things.

Pretenders vs Contenders

Pretenders show up on test day without studying. They are constantly late for the important matters in their lives. They miss appointments, fail to get things in on time and blame everybody and everything for their shortcomings. The weather, traffic, their computer, voicemail, and the day of the week all play a major factor in pretender's inability to meet the challenges of life. Life's challenges are the enemy of the pretender. Instead of teaching them to become better, life teaches them surrender and defeat.

Contenders however, are very different. The first thing you notice about a contender is that they are prepared. They arrive early. They ask questions. They do the homework, fieldwork and whatever it takes. They take pride in their work habits and their accomplishments. They focus on results and not excuses. When faced with challenges of life, pretenders shrink, and contenders grow. Life is test of your determination to get what you want out of life. It will present roadblocks, detours, storms and disasters to deter you from your course.

"Life challenges are not supposed to paralyze you they are suppose to help you discover who you are".

Bernice Johnson Reagon

Your character is developed through your struggles. Just like the butterfly must fight its way out of the cocoon in order to build the strength in its wings to fly.

"The truth is our finest moments are most likely to occur when we are feeling deeply uncomfortable, unhappy or unfulfilled. For it is only in such moments, propelled by our discomfort, that we are likely to step out of our own ruts, and start searching for different ways and truer answers."

Unknown

When obstacles appear, your goal is getting close. Will you pass the test or give up? Are you a contender or just a pretender? Obstacles are the things you see when you take your eyes off your goals.

In search of Excellence

There is one perfect being and that is GOD. Our mission on earth is to pursue those GODLIKE qualities within us. While no one is perfect, we all can become better. When you are in the process of being better, you become excellent. Excellence comes from the Latin, ex-, out of and "cellere" which means to rise; to be better or greater than.

Excellence in motion is excelling which is a verb - an action word. It's the process of being better. When you excel you go beyond and become greater than you were. You move to the next level. When you are doing this intentionally, you are manifesting your destiny.

Who you are and what you are is decided by what you do in the next instant? You control that; not others. **Frederick Douglas** was born in bondage. However, he was not a slave in his mind. If **Frederick Douglas** had let others define him, he could not have achieved what he did in history. People like Tubman, Booker T, Carver, Ali, Douglas, King, and Obama are icons in the history of America. Some people may have said at the time, what they accomplished was impossible.

NOTHING IS IMPOSSIBLE

Impossible is a dare. Impossible is not the truth. What people say is impossible today will become a reality tomorrow. Many years ago, flying was impossible now we are landing on the moon. Years ago, if someone said, people will be able to communicate with others by talking to a little box in their hand, someone would have said impossible. Today, young children have their own cell-phones. The word "impossible" was created to challenge those people whose mission is to make the impossible - possible.

Look at the word "Impossible". It says, "I'm possible" In order to change the "impossible" into that which is "possible" you must have vision.

"Impossible is just a big word thrown around by small men who find it easier to live the world they have been given, rather than to explore the power they have to change it. Impossible is not a fact. It is an opinion. Impossible is not a declaration. It is a dare. Impossible is potential. Impossible is temporary. Impossible is nothing."

John Maxwell

"I am not more gifted than the average human being. If you know anything about history, you would know that is so--what hard times I had in studying and the fact that I do not have a memory like some other people do... I am just more curious than the average person and I will not give up on a problem until I have found the proper solution. This is one of my greatest satisfactions in life--solving problems--and the harder they are, the more satisfaction do I get out of them. Maybe you could consider me a bit more patient in continuing with my problem than is the average human being. Now, if you understand what I have just told you, you see that it is not a matter of being more gifted but a matter of being more curious and maybe more patient until you solve a problem."

Albert Einstein

Be Magnificent! Exceed Your Expectations

BONUS FOR READERS – Let's keep in touch. Go to
www.michaelricespeaks.com and sign up.   Got questions, write me at
theConnector@verizon.net.

Chapter Five

<u>Getting in the Zone</u>

Do you have a beat to your life? Are you moving in a rhythm? All successful individuals have a rhythm to their life. Like the Bass player sets the beat, the quarterback calls the play, the drill sergeant bellows a cadence; successful individuals set up a rhythm in their lives. Once you establish a rhythm, things move swiftly and easily. Your life has a beat. When you are really flowing with the beat of life, you are in the Zone.

Lack of rhythm to your life can cause everything to become confusing and chaotic. Nothing seems to go right, and your life is out of sync. Your team members and associates can't help you because you are inconsistent and out of alignment.

I remember when I was in the military my days were filled with rhythm. During boot camp we marched to a cadence everyday. We would march to breakfast, lunch and dinner. The cadence made it easier for all of us to move as one. In order to keep us together, one person would yell out the cadence.

Rhythm is a management tool

Developing a rhythm can help you manage your contacts, team and organization. Once a common rhythm is developed everyone can move as a unit. Common goals equal common direction.

Consistent Action creates Momentum

Successful Individuals schedule regular team meetings and sends out informational emails thereby creating a steady beat of communication. It puts everyone in step with each other. As **Stuart R. Levine**, author of **"The Six Fundamentals of Success"** states, "the manager sets the pace and the team keeps the rhythm."

Getting into your Zone is more than just establishing a rhythm although that's a start in the right direction. The Zone is defined in Sports Medicine as "a state of maximum physical, mental and psychological performance achieved by star athletes". When you are in your zone, you will flow with life. There is a mind to body connection that puts you in your groove and life becomes easy and effortless. We have seen people in the zone. Once **Michael Jordan** was in the Zone, he became unstoppable on the court. **Bill Gates** got into the Zone and become a multi billionaire. Tiger Woods in his Zone became unbeatable. **Barack Obama** got into his Zone and became President of the United States. Highly successful people find their inner beat and get in their Zone.

Getting in the zone is an awesome state of mind, body and spirit; whether you are on the basketball court, the golf course, playing the market, networking or running for office. You just keep hitting shot after shot, making the right choices and meeting the right people. When you are in the zone, you become magnetic. You are not only able to seize opportunities, but you attract them as well.

How to get into your Zone!

1. **Practice your craft**- Only through constant repetition do you achieve peak performance. Practice mentally, physically and spiritually. (Set aside practice time everyday)

2. **Meditate and visualize yourself achieving your goals several times a day**. Make sure you incorporate not only the visual image, but also the emotional joy, confidence and feeling of victory you will experience while reaching your goals.

3. **Make it a habit of making phone calls and sending updates via email.** This will help you establish your rhythm and your co-workers will appreciate the consistent flow of information. You will appear dependable, resourceful and supportive.

4. **Create rituals and systems in your life**. Put things on a schedule. Set up a routine. Random

meetings upset the flow. Regular meetings help people know what to expect. Regular scheduling will help manage your time and the time of others.

The more you are consistent with your actions, the closer you get to your Zone. **Magnificent people** are consistent in their actions and it translates in consistent outcomes. The player who practices going to the hoop becomes better and better in every game. After consistent practice, they stop thinking about the shot. Like the slogan from Nike, "Just do it" infers an instinctive action that does not require analysis just correct action. You can train your mind and body to act as one. Whether you are on the court or in the office, your actions become the ball and your goals are the hoop. Become the Ball and you will be in your Zone.

Chapter Six

Your Magic Words

Your mind is one of the most powerful tools you could ever possess. Unfortunately, we only tap into 10% our mind's potential. The percentage will be lower for some individuals. When your mind is utilized fully, you become 100 times more powerful than any computer. Think about it, while driving your car, your mind is operating hundreds of applications including: sight, hearing, taste, smell. Not to mention, running your heart, kidney, brain, and thousands of other biological functions without you thinking about it.

If you can learn how to manage your mind, you can overcome bad habits, create confidence, lift yourself from depression and create a new reality for yourself.

Here's one technique that allow you to access the powers of your mind. It's called the "**The Magic Word.**"

The technique is based on the process called anchoring. If you have ever been happy, sad, fearful or confident, you can anchor the feeling and reproduce it. Think about it. Have you ever been in a great mood and suddenly on the radio a certain song came on? You instantly feel sad and depressed. You remember a time, when your heart was broken. The song causes you to reminisce about a certain person, a place and feeling.

On the contrary, can you remember a time, when you weren't happy or enthused? Then a certain song came on the radio and now you are feeling energetic and motivated. Your body wants to dance, and your thoughts are bright and hopeful. The Song is the anchor. When you heard the song, a picture entered your mind. This was followed by a feeling or emotion. The feeling and emotion combined changed your mood and affected your state of mind.

I will show you how to anchor your mood to a word and gesture. Your magic word connected with an action and a feeling will give you the ability to create confident and happiness at will.

YOUR MAGIC WORD

To create this magic word, please follow these steps.

1. Find a quiet place where you will not be interrupted. Sit in a comfortable chair. Both feet on the floor. Don't cross your legs.

2. Relax; count down from 20 to 1. As you count down feel your muscles relaxing from head to your toes. Imagine your body is filled with water. As you count down, imagine that the water is draining out of your big toe. As its drains from your head,

down your neck to your shoulders, arms, chest; feel your muscles relax. Your body should go limp as you count down.

Once you get to 1. If any muscles still have tension focus on it. Imagine a spotlight on it; now count down 5, 4, 3, 2,1.

3.   Once you are completely relaxed, imagine a mirror image of yourself. Think back to a time when you were filled with confidence. One of those days when you felt unstoppable.

See how you are dressed. Imagine you are in your most confident state. Shoulders back, relaxed yet ready for action. You are alert and ready for any challenge. See yourself interacting confidently with others. You are walking and talking with supreme confidence. You see people impressed with you. They complement your dress and style.

Get the feeling within your body. Once you got the feeling associate it to a word or a phase such as

- It's On!
- I got the power
- I am the power!
- Power on

Now then snap your fingers. This is creating an anchor. Now do this exercise at least 5 times to anchor it to your self-conscious.

Important: You must feel the emotion of confidence. Visualize yourself in a confident mood. Feel the power, the magnetism and force on attraction within. Then say your magic word – **"It's On"**.

Feel the surge of power within your entire body. Your mind is clarified. The body feels strong and powerful. You are going to see the picture of yourself and say your magic words five times. Each time you will feel yourself becoming more and more powerful and confident.

Use this technique when you going to connect with new people. Use before a sale or when you are recruiting for your organization. Use it when you are going for the big speech, interview or presentation. Say your magic words and snap your fingers. Activate your confident state. People will feel your energy and you will affect them. You will see your personal power in action. The more you do it, the easier it becomes to access your power state.

BONUS FOR READERS - Want to keep current with the latest ideas, tips and advice on how you can be the best you can? Visit www.theconnectornetwork.com and sign up. You also can Text - B-Mag to theConnector@verizon.net for free videos and our social digest subscription.

Be Magnificent! Exceed Your Expectations

Chapter Seven

SUDDEN IMPACT: MAKING A GREAT FIRST IMPRESSION

" You never get a second chance to make a good first impression," stated Will Roger. This quote is amazingly true. It does not matter whether you are going on an interview, making a new acquaintance, showing up for court or presenting at community or business meetings, your first impression is a lasting one.

Let's face the fact that we all want to make a good first impression. People make decisions about you based upon their impression of you in the first few seconds of meeting you. Your clothes, body language, walk, demeanor and mannerism add up the person's initial opinion of you. The good news is if your first impression is positive it can lead to a job, acceptance, respect and more. The bad news is if your impression is negative, it can have lasting effects and sometimes will become impossible to undo.

After attending hundreds of meetings and networking events, I have developed some helpful tips that helped me become more successful in my personal "**urban networking**". During my early days of networking, I was intimidated in the room full of successful professionals. This was before I learned how to identify my personal assets, qualities and talents that made me a unique individual. When I learned how to articulate my personal qualities, I focused on opening conversations with confidence. Eventually, I developed strategies for developing successful mutually beneficial relationships.

In this chapter, you will learn some techniques for creating a high impact first impression. You will learn how questions can open new contacts and aid in creating rapport. One of the key elements in making a good first impression is your initial presentation. Your opening statements should be high impact and memorable. Once you have opened conversation, use key questions to extend the communications and deepen rapport. How you end your conversation with your new contacts is just as important. A strong closing conversation will extend your good impression and have a strong and memorable impact.

VALIDATION

Opening a conversation with a new contact is paying them an honest compliment. An appeal to a person's ego goes a long way after opening the door and establishing a rapport with the possibility of future collaborations.

Regardless if you are a youth or an adult, there is a child inside each one of us seeking approval and validation.

Your compliments touch the child within and give your new contact a sense of well-being. It is almost magical how compliments create resourceful states that can lead to the development of successful relationships.

KEY QUESTIONS OPEN THE DOOR

The compliment can be in the form of a question regarding their expertise, profession, clothing, jewelry, experience, etc. The idea is to stimulate interest and the need to respond from your prospect. Nothing will bring that out more than by talking about something they find of interest.

Some examples below:

How long have you been doing community work? I know you have some interesting stories.

- That's an interesting tie, where did you get it?
- Great suit, is it from Boyd's? (Macy's, Lord and Taylor's, etc.)
- I have always been interested in the stock market. How did you happen to get involved in the markets?
- Everyone is interested in the housing market. I bet you have some real insight into how it works?
- So you're a nurse? Is that what you wanted to become when you grew up?
- You're a teacher. I know you have some interesting stories regarding your kids.

The secret of this technique is to keep the conversation on what your prospect is interested in and not what you are interested in. Keep in mind that you are also gathering information to be used when you do your follow up phone call and subsequent conversations.

If you know nothing about a person's background, focus on their appearance. Comment on their shoes, dress, purse, tie, scarf or jewelry. You will be remembered as an interesting conversationalist and a great person.

Other tips for a good first impression are:

- **Dress for Success**- How you dress expresses who you are?

- **Hygiene** – This is extremely important, and this includes deodorant, breath odor, and general cleanliness.

- **Grooming** – Fresh haircuts, salon styled hairdos and manicured nails states your game is tight.

- **Style** – This is how you put yourself together based upon your own self-image. Tattoos and piercings distract people from your true self.

- **Your smile** – Key to presenting yourself as a positive, open and friendly individual.

- **Confidence** – Your ability to express yourself, your personality and interact with high value with others.

- **Positive Attitude**- if you initially make negative statements, people will think you are basically a negative person.

- **Etiquette**- your manners, courtesy and social skills are outward expressions of your core self.

In this Chapter we will cover the elements of making a great first impression. We will provide you with the personal factors for establishing memorable initial meetings. We will identify the three types of relationships and the importance of identifying your prospect's primary motivation.

Question: When you are first meeting a prospective contact what four factors combined contributed to high impact first impression?

Answer:

- **Firm handshake**
- **A dazzling smile**
- **Professional presence**
- **An interest creating introduction**

Handshake

A firm handshake shows the contact you are confident and outgoing.

A dazzling smile

Smiles are disarming and powerful. They put a person at ease. In addition to showing that you are approachable and open.

Your Professional presence

Shows you have pride in your appearance. Your presence is also positive body language and upright posture.

An interest creating introduction

By beginning your approach to a new stranger with an interesting and engaging conversation, you show confidence, intelligence, professionalism and openness. The initial meeting should be about you learning as much as possible about the new contact. Contrary to popular belief, you tell you prospect the least about you. Instead, you take the opportunity to learn as much as you can about the person.

Ask relevant questions

People feel very flattered when you appear to be interested in who they are and what they do. However, do not interrogate them. Ask relevant questions to provide you with the information you are seeking.

When you were younger was this the profession you desired?

What did you want to become when you grew up?

In social/business settings sometimes you must determine what type of relationship the individual is seeking. By asking the right questions, you can to qualify them for the type of relationship you are seeking.

There are three types of relationships:

Emotional – This relationship is based upon friendship, love and attachment.

Financial – This relationship is based in business interactions that could be official business as in provider, consumer, co-worker, partnership, collaborations, or social business as in "sugar daddy" or personal sponsorship relationship between men and women. Co-worker relationships fall under financial because the goal of making money falls under this category.

Physical – This sexual relationship is based in which the parties are seeking sexual satisfaction as the primary reason for connecting.

Many relationships have a combination of the emotional, financial and physical aspect. However, a good networker determines what the primary motivation of his or her prospect is initially. Many social relationships fail because the participants failed to understand the motivation of the partner. If your partner primary interest in connecting with you is monetary and your primary motivation is emotional or physical. You may be able to establish a mutually beneficial relationship if both participants' desires are met.

There are many relationships where the man or woman is looking for someone to take care of them financially in exchange for emotional or a physical relationship. In fact, many older people enter relationships with finances as the primary common interests. However, relationships fail when individuals do not understand the motivation of the significant other. Entering a relationship with someone whose primary goal is finances and you are seeking an emotionally motivated individual will not work. Networkers seek to combine the financial and emotional aspect together creating relationship in which the participants feel loyalty, commitment, respect and sense of connection with each other.

How to start a Conversation with new people?

You finally convinced yourself to attend one of those networking events. Your colleagues and friend tell you that you have to get out and network. You realize now in your career that mixing and mingling with key people is essential to getting the awards, promotions and resources to become successful in your industry.

You identify a key group of individuals who you know you want to meet. You would love to be apart of that inner circle. You move in to the group who are already engaged in a conversation. Everyone stops talking and looks at you as if they are waiting on your opening statement. The clocks ticks and you freeze. You can't think of what to say and you even forget to introduce yourself. The second passes, the conversation continues; without you.

You punked yourself

Have you ever had this paralyzing experience or one similar? Breaking the ice and connecting with people can become very intimidating. However, practicing with confidence can overcome all those frustrating moments.

The key to confidence is competence.

You want competence in your conversations and relationship building skills. Knowing what to say and how to connect with new people is vitally important.

When we talk about networking one of the key challenges that people shared was that they did not know how to start conversations with new people. What to say is a key question. In this chapter, we will address the challenge in seven simple steps. Before I provide you with these steps, lets first address a key ingredient in your repertoire. That is your mindset. As **a Magnificent individual**, you must see yourself as a walking asset. Before you go out and attempt to connect with others, you should start with a self-assessment. This assessment should focus on your personal assets. In other words, what do you bring to the table?

Start by listing qualities you possess such as compassion, funny, outgoing, resourceful, helpful, smart, good friend, musically inclined etc. Think about the positive impact you had on your friends, children, family, clients, and patients. Add what you bring to the table in business, friendship and as a co-worker. Now list your different qualities or skills such as analytical, detail oriented, a people person or a driver personality who get things done.

The purpose of this exercise is for you to point out to yourself that you are asset to any relationship, organization or conversation. Once you completed your inventory; there are a couple more dimensions to your mindset.

1. **Have a positive outlook** - No one wants to hang around Ms Fumby or Mr. Negative. People like being around others who feel good about their life. Keep in mind, you can feel just as good about your plans for future as your accomplishments. Remember if you feel good about yourself, its magnetic. People sense it and that's attractive.

2. **Don't take it personal** – You can attempt to initiate a conversation with someone who is having a bad day and they will response negatively. Regardless of who you are or what you say it will not have an impact on someone who is preoccupied with his or her own problems; so, move on. You always want to set your sights on bringing positive people into your life. Everyone will not be receptive. That is not a reflection on you nor is it your responsibility to change their outlook. Move on to your next prospect quickly before you get sucked into a negative vibe or create a negative state.

3. **Don't be concerned with the outcome.** Once you become a skilled Networker, people will flock to you and initiate conversations. Moreover, don't worry about the outcome of your initial contact with new people. Consider every encounter as practice. If you were practicing playing baseball and you got depressed every time you missed the ball. You would mentally and emotionally run yourself down. Think about it, Phillies star Homerun hitter Ryan Howard strikes out a lot. When he gets in his zone the ball is out of the park. If Howard got depressed every time, he missed the ball, he would never become a major star in his sport.

4. **Make it a game to find something in common with people you meet.** With each encounter with new people, make it a game to learn something about them. Always seek to find what you and that person have in common. The key to rapport with people is finding out what you have in common. One of the key psychological tools used by advertisers in marketing is something called "Liking". You know liking is being used when you begin to identify with the person in the picture or in the commercial. They look like you and have the same concerns and desires as you. In selling to young people they use teen-agers. In selling to senior citizens, you can bet there will be a gray-haired man or woman in the commercial. In selling to African Americans not only will there be black people in the commercial, but the background music will either represent, jazz, R&B or hip-hop.

5. **Be a people person** – Someone who is described as people person genuinely likes people. They are concerned with their feelings and they ask questions and they make statements regarding other people's well being. The rule is simple. If you want friends be friendly. If you want to create exciting mutually beneficial relationships, let people know. Be open and honest. Get out of

your head and out your own way. Your mission is to create positive relationships. You only can do that by being aggressive, outgoing and friendly. The "**Law of Attraction**" states that which you send out comes back to you.

6. **Share a little about yourself** – This will open doors for you. People prefer to engage with people who they know about. I know many times, I have met people who because I was initially reserved, believed I was stand offish and closed. However, once they got to know me, they told me they had gotten the wrong impression. Share your passions. Share your personal stories and people with share with you.

7. **Make compliments**- People love to be validated. After all, wouldn't you rather be around individuals who recognize your worth and value. People, who dress well, spend time and effort in carefully selecting their clothes and perfecting their style. Their work is rewarded when you compliment them on their outfits. Supervisors get more out of their employees when they motivate them through sincere and honest compliments.

8. **Be Informed** – Be able to talk on many topics such as local news, sports, politics, etc.

9. **Set goals to meet people to build your circle.** The more people you meet the better you become in building rapport.

10. **Always exit on a high note.** Your first and last impression counts. Always try to end a conversation on a high note. Leave your new contact with the desire to talk with you again.

BONUS FOR READERS – You are doing good. Want to keep current with the latest ideas, tips and advice on how you can be the best you can? Visit www.theconnectornetwork.com and sign up. You also can Text - B-Mag to theConnector@verizon.net for free videos and our social digest subscription.

Chapter Eight

HANDLING DIFFICULT PEOPLE

This chapter was originally entitled, "Dealing with the co-worker from Hell." Have you ever had a co-worker that just got on your last nerve? They always seem to be doing something to irritate you. Maybe they didn't know their job, so you had to work harder to compensate for their deficiencies. Maybe they really didn't want to work so they would just show up everyday, mess up production and distract others. Perhaps they didn't like you or considered you a rival and they were are trying to get your job.

A survey by Careerbuilder.com of 2500 workers in 2006 found that 77% of workers felt stressed out.

The top stressor was: **Difficult coworkers**

As a successful individual, you must learn how to deal with all types of people. While a lot of your networking will take place outside your job, many of your successful contacts will be developed at the workplace. People will judge you based upon how you deal with difficult situations and people.

So how do you deal with difficult co-workers or colleagues without dragging them outside and beating the slop out of them? I am going to give you some steps to overcome the desire to choke the living ...... out of your coworkers.

1. **First control yourself.** The first impulse for dealing with a difficult person is to react. Sometimes you react without thinking and then regret your actions.

Imagine: Your co-worker does or says something you don't like. You punch him in the mouth. YOU get fired. They continue to work and eventually take your job.

"Check yourself before you wreck yourself".

This scenario does not sound good; does it? In order to gain control of this situation, the first thing you want to do is check yourself. Relax and keep your voice low and modulated. Think out your response and become strategic. A colleague of mine told me about a co-worker who was fiercely jealous of him. When he got a promotion as the head of his unit, a memo was sent out informing everyone of his good fortune. His co-worker took the memo and wrote Bulls**t across the front, made copies and distributed them into employees' inboxes. Although he knew the person who did it, he could not prove it. So, he had to let it ride. The person continued to pull childish stunts and eventually everyone realized how unprofessional they were. Eventually they were transferred to another department.

Now if my colleague had reacted and confronted the person, he would have given his opponent exactly what they wanted. Negative people cannot hide who they are no more than a good person. The real you will always show up and show out.

2. **Ignore the behavior and deal with the issues.** By focusing on the issues, you avoid personal conflicts and emotional reactions. When confronting a co-worker about a behavior remember to separate the behavior from the person.

A co-worker always leaves the lunchroom a mess with their trash and garbage. Avoid calling them names. Don't say, "You are such a slob. You always leave the lunchroom a mess." Their reaction may be "Who you are calling a slob?" Focus on the issue. Do say, "according to work conduct rules, it is everyone responsibility to clean up after themselves. Don't you prefer a clean and sanitary lunchroom?

"Am I not destroying my enemies when I make a friend of them." Abe Lincoln

3. **Utilize positive motivation verses negative criticism.** Don't hate. Congratulate and communicate the behavior you want to see and don't reinforce the behavior you don't want. "You are a good worker and better than the work you have been performing. Here is how the report should look. Do you need some help?"

I attended a Personal Development training called, "Investment in Excellence." The performance coach Lou Tice, the founder talked about "coaching forward". He stated we often affirm negative behavior with criticism, which reinforces the negative behavior. "Remember the more we affirm the behavior in a person we don't want, the more they become like it" stated Lou Tice. He suggests, when we see the behavior we don't like in that person, what if we tell them, "I see you as being…." and you go on to describe the way you'd like to see them. Instead of telling them, "there you go again". "You been doing it for all your life, you'll never change". What you might say is "Stop it you're too good for that…." and you go on to describe the way you positively see them or want them to become.

4. **Model the behavior you want to encourage**. I had a block captain on my street that was so frustrated at some neighbors not cleaning their sidewalk that she swept it herself. The ending result was the neighbor was so embarrassed by this 70-year-old lady sweeping their sidewalk, that they begin cleaning their walkway without being told.

5. **Don't be Mr. Right all the time**. – Okay, so you are smart and successful. You don't have to be right all the time. (Even if you are). Let others win the argument. People hate co-workers who think they know everything. They talk about them behind their backs and celebrate when Mr. Know-it-all makes an error. Become the person people go to when they need help. Don't become the person they dread asking for assistance.

"It is far more impressive when others discover your good qualities without your help"

Judith Martin.

6. Be open to suggestions - Believe it or not other people have good ideas. Successful individuals are open to new and different ideas. They can use the best suggestions to get the job done. When you utilize other co-workers' suggestions, they feel validated. In this instance, they are more likely to help and support to your projects. This is a win-win.

"Better to light a candle, then curse the darkness"

Eleanor Roosevelt.

7. Be the Light – The person in charge lacks leadership skills. You don't have to be in the fore front to lead just be support; don't make your boss look bad. You are better off letting the boss be the boss.

A supervisor and co-workers are standing outside their building when they notice a small unique bottle in the grass. One of the workers picks it up and dusts it off. Suddenly a genie appears and tells them he will grant each one of them one wish. The first worker says, "Me first- me first." He steps forward and wishes to be on a beautiful beach in Jamaica surrounded by beautiful women who desire him. The genie snaps his fingers and the coworker disappears.

The second worker jumps up and says," Me next!" She asks for a beautiful house by the beach filled with money. The Genie snaps his finger and she disappear. The Genie turns to the supervisor and asks for his wish. The supervisor says I wish that both my employees were back at their desks in 5 minutes.

Moral of the story: Always let the boss go first.

Being part of team means you support the person in charge. You will get better results by convincing your supervisors that you are looking out for their best interests. When you are successful on the job, share the credit. The **Magnificent individual** shares the credit and rewards. He knows that it's because of his supportive network that he can win.

"There are two kinds of people on a job. There are those who do the work and those who take the credit. Be apart of the first group, there is less competition."

On a final note, when facing an individual whose plotting on taking your job.

"It's not the size of the dog in the fight, it's the size of the fight in the dog."
Randolph W. Cameron, author of "The Minority Executives" handbook states you should take the following steps:

- o **Get all the facts – Don't act on gossip or rumors.**
- o **Access the political strength of your opponent.**
- o **Take positive and aggressive action.**
- o **Protect your territory by ensuring your work is up to date, your performance is good, and your staff is willing to support you.**

- o **Utilize your corporate mentors both inside and outside your company.**
- o **Reinforce your position by conducting serious networking.**

Remember if you cannot think of a difficult co-worker on your job than you may the problem.

In the end, you create your own reality. Don't give your power to someone else. Do not dwell on trying to change someone else but concentrate on changing yourself.

> **"How far you go in life depends on you being tender with the young, compassionate with the aged, sympathetic with the striving and tolerant with the weak and the strong. Because someday in life, you will have been all of these",**
>
> George Washington Carver.

BONUS FOR READERS - Want to keep current with the latest ideas, tips and advice on how you can be the best you can? Visit www.theconnectornetwork.com and sign up.

Chapter Nine

GAME

"You have to learn the rules of the GAME then you have to play better than anyone else".

Albert Einstein

Throughout history the term "**GAME**" has been used to describe situations, attitudes, skills and strategies. In this Chapter, when we talk about "**GAME**" we are not referring to organized activities that are played with a ball. We are not talking about family and friends' activities played at a party or what your children do during recess.

The **GAME**, we are referring to is much deeper and significant in your life. Every great leader or successful businessperson has learned the **GAME** and became excellent at playing it.

This chapter is about successful individuals who play the "**Game.**" Each player knows they must become knowledgeable of their game in order to be successful.

Webster defines **GAME** as a plan of action. It's a process with a set of rules that are followed. When you are "**ahead of the GAME**" you are winning, doing well or thriving. If you are "**off your GAME**" you are performing poorly, doing badly, or failing. In order to "**play the**

GAME" you must behave properly, act according to custom and do what is expected.

Your **Game Plan** is your map for exploring the world called LIFE. This was written to help you formulate your approach to dealing with life on your own terms.

In sports, individuals who become skilled at the game are the ones that practice consistently. Through repetition and challenging themselves they move themselves to the "**Top of the GAME**".

Life is the only game in which the object of the **GAME** is to learn the rules. In fact, if you decide you want to have a higher level of skill called **GAME,** you need to establish a worthwhile goal for anyone seeking to achieve success.

"When I first started flirting with the hustle, failure became my ex; now I am engaged to the GAME and married to success "

Lil Wayne, millionaire rapper.

In fact, **Voltaire**, a famous French author and philosopher said it best" Each player must accept the cards life deals to him or her, but once they are in hand, he or she alone must decide how to play the cards in order to win the **GAME**."

Confidence

A key ingredient in having **GAME** is confidence. Confidence in a person attracts other people to them like a magnet. Would you love to move and talk with the confidence and vitality of Denzel Washington or Idris Elba? Do you see the aura that surrounds these individuals? It's magnetic, authentic, and genuine.

"One of the important keys to success is self-confidence.
An important key to self -confidence is preparation".

Arthur Ashe

A successful individual gives off the impression
and demeanor of importance and success. They express it
through their dress and their social poise. Think of the
successful individuals in your field. Do they exhibit these
qualities?

Focus on the positive

By focusing on their positive traits, they are able to
live dynamically. Successful individuals concentrate on
things he or she can improve – whether they are trying a
new hairstyle, working out, buying a new wardrobe, going
back to school or pursuing a better job. They know that
working on self-improvement is a great self -esteem
builder.

Affirmations

One of the keys of developing your self-confidence
is writing your own affirmations that give you power. In
metaphysics, it is believed that there is a supreme
consciousness that is a source of power and knowledge.
Advanced practitioners can tap that power. They become
one with the source through meditation, affirmations and
visualization. By affirming their goals and seeing their
personal success in advance, they can actualize their goals.

By practicing visualization and affirming positive
statements, the individual is able overcome limiting beliefs

that chain them to the past and crippling behaviors. Practice improves performance. Practice in empowers the practitioner with mental programming focusing on their goals.

Here is a powerful affirmation to recite daily.

I will always seek to be greater than I am. I must exceed myself. In each successive move, act, test, interaction or thought, I will be more magnificent than the one before. I am what I am now, but in an hour, I will surpass who I am presently. In everything I do I must exercise more power to exceed myself.

The outcome of this affirmation will be realized in time. In order to effectively assimilate this affirmation into your self-conscious, you should recite it every day, in the morning and evening before you go to sleep. You should visualize the success you desire in life. See images of you succeeding. Imagine yourself receiving awards, your boss giving you a promotion; you are purchasing your dream home or meeting and connecting with the love of your life.

As you visualize and recite the affirmation to yourself, feel the emotions of victory, love, and accomplishment. Imagine how you would feel at that moment and experience that emotion.

Exercise:

Write down this affirmation and place by your bed. Before you go to sleep at night, put yourself in a relaxed state and read the affirmation over and over. Imagine living the life you choose and passionately experiencing it.

When you wake up in the morning repeat the process. In addition, sometime during the day find some quiet place and repeat the process. Over time, the power of this affirmation will assimilate into your subconscious mind. You find yourself more motivated and your performance improving.

BONUS FOR READERS - Want to keep current with the latest ideas, tips and advice on how you can be the best you can? Visit www.theconnectornetwork.com and sign up. You also can Text - B-Mag to theConnector@verizon.net for free videos and our social digest subscription.

Chapter Ten

HOW TO CHANGE YOUR SOCIAL STATUS: BIRDS OF A FEATHER

Three idiots who were walking down the road when they came upon what seemed like a hug pile of dog feces. The first idiot put his eye in it and says, "looks like poop." The second idiot put his nose in it and said, "smells like poop." The last one put his tongue in it and said, "tastes like poop." They all looked at each other and said, "Lucky we did not step in it."

"Its is better to travel alone then with a bad companion."
African proverb

Be mindful of the company you keep. If you feel you are the smartest person on your team, you need a new team. This is because you will either cosign on bad ideas by others or you will never respect their input. In the first case, yes, it is easier to let others do the thinking for you. However, at the end of the day, you will be responsible for your circumstances. In the latter, if you think you are smarter than your colleagues, no matter what advice they provide, you will discount it because you did not think of it. In addition, you will never become more successful than they people who you associate. Whether or not you accept this concept or not, you adopt the limitations of your friends. It's been said, you make within $5,000 of your closest associates. If you want to increase your income, began connecting with individuals with significant wealth.

Finally, birds of a feather flock together. Decide today whether you want to become just another pigeon or if you are going fly like an Eagle.

In many of our Leadership Development workshops, I have been asked on numerous occasions. Is there anything, one can do to immediately change their lifestyle or direction? I reply individuals dissatisfied with the current course of their life, do have an option.

If you want to immediately elevate yourself and put yourself closer to real success? The answer is simple; Change the people with whom you associate.

The phase, **"Birds of a feather flock together"** is not just a saying, it's a universal law. If you want to elevate your standard of living, then elevate the standard of people with whom you spend your time.

Here's the **Magnificent individual's** rule, "Winners hang with winners. Losers hang with losers. The positive hang with the positive and the negative want company." **Misery loves company**.

I observed this common factor while working with parents with children who exhibited delinquent behaviors. These children usually duplicated their peer group. Truant children associated with truant youth. Delinquent children associated with other delinquents. Think about it, if all your child's friends ditch school and smoke marijuana, then your child is more than likely to play hooky and smoke weed. Your child's peer group displays common traits of its members.

Parents have been successful in changing their children behavior by involving them in activities and programs where children practice positive habits. When the child identifies with the group, they adopt the groups habits. Adults are no different. We adopt the habits, activities and behaviors of people who we frequent the most. Our actions and vocabulary changes to match the people we come into contact daily. Be careful of the people who you associate. Your circle of influence can be your vehicle for self-elevation or the cement shoes that sends you to the bottom of the river.

Misery loves company

In the social work arena, I have worked extensively with drug addicts. One thing I observed that it appeared that many addicts were unhappy when one of their fellow addicts attempted to quit drugs. In fact, they would take every opportunity to cause that person to fail by offering free drugs or using drugs around them. I venture to say that for those individuals to see someone quit using drugs would mean they would have to look at themselves and take responsibility for their actions.

Enablers

Often in families, we found people we call "enablers." While they profess that they want their son, brother, sister to change, they provide money, food, etc., that allow the person to continue in their destructive behavior. While consciously, enablers may think they are doing the drug addict a favor by providing them with money and other needs. They may subconsciously want the addict to remain in their addictive mindset. Enablers get off on being the rescuer. This allows them to maintain their sense of superiority and power over the addict. Children don't learn how to walk on their own if their parent's keeps holding them up. These enabling behaviors weaken their ability to learn on their own.

In the case of butterflies, during their metamorphosis they must break out of their cocoon. If you assist them, they will not develop the wing strength they will enable them to fly. So, by helping them you sabotage their growth.

Are your friends like you?

Think about the people who you associate. How successful are they? Are they supportive of your goals or do they redirect the conversation to themselves when you talk about your achievements? In relation to your goals are they the people who you would associate with if you achieved your goals.

Do they share your values and believe in the same principles you do? If you are developing a higher spiritual self, then you don't want to spend a lot of time with people who are spiritually corrupt.

"Blessed is the man that walketh not in the counsel of the ungodly, nor standeth in the way of sinners, nor sitteth in the seat of the scornful"

Psalm 1:1

If there is an inconsistency in your personal circle, you may need to reevaluate your associations. Don't get me wrong; I'm not saying you should drop all your lifelong friends who are not on the social economic level you have established as your goal. However, I am saying cultivate the social environment of your goals. When we practice visualizing our goals, we see the people, the places and the environments that we will associate, frequent and live within.

Look in the mirror

Your friends and associates are reflections of yourself. Sometimes you don't have to look in the mirror to see yourself. Just look at your friends and you will see a true representation of who you are. While your friend may not be on the same financial level as yourself, they may have high moral and spiritual values you admire. Look at your friends and associates holistically. Take into consideration, their family, educational, intellectual, spiritual and financial values and attributes.

In a recent workshop with Performance Coach **Early Jackson**, and CEO of New Directions Coaching, he stated, "according to research, a person makes within $6,000 dollars of their peer group." This makes sense especially in the US where we have class systems such lower class, middle class, upper classes. Americans tend to live and associate with individuals in their own income levels.

Finally, if you want to change your social environment, outcomes and opportunities, become selective of the people who you spend time with. Take the following steps

1. Set goals on spending time with individuals who occupy the positions and lifestyle you aspire.

2. Identify the habits and social venue in which you wish to become part of your lifestyle.

3. Visualize the people, places and activities that you wish to duplicate in your life.

4. Create vision boards from magazine clippings of your desired lifestyle.

5. Go to places and events frequently where the people who fit the lifestyle you desire.

6. Utilize the networking techniques in making contact and establishing mutually beneficial relationships.

Homework

Write down your personal networking goals. Who do you want in your circle of influence? Who would you want on your success team? Identify the type of people who represent your success model. Look at their personal values in the categories of spirituality, morality, family, education and financial. What values are you reaching for and who can share with you their personal knowledge of how you can achieve them?

BONUS FOR READERS - Want to keep current with the latest ideas, tips and advice on how you can be the best you can? Visit www.theconnectornetwork.com and sign up. You also can Text - B-Mag to theConnector@verizon.net for free videos and our social digest subscription.

Chapter Eleven

Be Magnificent!

The key to exceeding your expectations is overcoming your self-limiting and self-imposed beliefs.

Living in the Matrix

Believe it or not, we all live within a matrix. The matrix is driven by the media, and other forces. From the time you can read and listen; you are being bombarded with messages. These messages tell you who you are. They tell you based upon what you own, where you live and who your parents are; where you fit into society. They also tell you that in order to be accepted or acceptable, you must change your hair, your style of dress, the people with who you associate, you must go to certain schools, get a certain level of education, drive a certain type of car and have certain view of the world.

In many cases, they dictate to you if you are not born into aristocracy, you should accept your place in society. Some messages are very subtle infused in commercials, news and in your favorite shows. Others are more blatant, and they forced on you by city, state and local government, advertisers and educational systems. I am not telling you all of this to depress you or to make you desperate, but the fact of the matter is if you don't realize how much and how intense the negative forces are impacting you. You will never change. You will never be happy. No matter how much money, power or things you own, you will never be satisfied.

You must open your eyes. Most of us live our entire lives with our eyes wide shut. We walk around thinking we see and understanding what is going on but, we really don't. Now there are times when we get a glimpse of the true reality, but we are quick to deny it. This is because it is not comfortable. It irritates us. Therefore, we reject it.

The Elephant Story

They train elephants in the circus. The story says that at an early age baby elephants are chained to giant posts implanted in the ground. The chains are strong enough to hinder the actions of a baby elephant. However as the elephant grows larger, the chains are replaced with ropes. A grown elephant with little or no effort easily breaks these ropes, but they don't. They don't because they are been trained from a young age about their limitations. They learn not to even test the bonds that keep them in check.

The Experiment

The other day, I watched one of those science shows. It talked about an experiment that was done on puppies. It sounded horrible but amazing knowledge was gained. In the experiment, puppies were placed in a metal cage with an opening at one end. From time to time different parts of the cage were electrified. The puppy would be literally dancing in the cage to avoid the electrical shock. Finally, they would escape through the opening.

The second part of the experiment was the puppies being placed in the cage with a harness. This harness would not allow them to move. The cage was again electrified. First the puppies struggled to get away from the charge. After several times, the puppies would give in and not try to avoid the charge. They accepted the situation.

In the final part of the experiment the same puppies were placed in the cage without the harness. The electrical charge was applied and even without the harness the puppies did not try to move. Even when the door was opened to allow them to exit, they did not attempt to avoid the pain. They acquiesced-consented without protest.

This is called, "**learned helplessness**". Most of us live in a state of **"learned helplessness"**. Some people express it by not voting in elections. Some people express by denying the existence of God. While others express it by not attempting to improve themselves or their conditions. People also use it as a reason not to go to school or to commit crime.

You see people everyday living in the streets and they have given up. Life has beaten them down. Some people live their entire lives in the worse possible conditions. They have the power to change but they don't. Why? Learned helplessness.

Many African Americans were conditioned to this state through slavery. There were times during the slavery era especially in the South, that the slaves on a plantation exceeded the size of the Slave owner's family and staff. In order to control this situation and avoid life-threatening uprisings, Slave masters realized they needed more than physical deterrents i.e., chains or fences. What they needed was a form of control that affected the desires and thinking of the slaves. They began to institute a form of psychological bondage that included "learned helplessness" and its effects today may be called "**Post-Traumatic Slave Disorder**".

Their electrified cage was replaced with slave masters whip and many forms of degradation, humiliation and subjugation that enslaved fathers, mothers and children suffered and witnessed. This systematic racism and oppression has resulted in many adaptive behaviors that originally were survival strategies that have now loss their contextual relevance.

This means that behaviors such as submissiveness, passiveness, non-assertiveness, repressed anger aka depression worked to help slaves survive. Mothers to keep their sons from being killed or maimed reinforce those behaviors. While the institution of slavery no longer exists the intergenerational effects still live on in many people. Many African Americans today have the intergenerational "learned helplessness" passed on from mother to child. Today, we still see this conditioning affecting the desires and aspirations of many people. Think about it, if it worked on this small group of people, why not try it out on the masses?

The point here is that everything is not what it seems. Your children are being taught and affected from their cartoons. The cartoons teach them status, classism, sexism, racism, age discrimination and more. Through their cartoons, they are taught to demoralize, discriminate and denigrate people, situations, countries and religions. In our educational systems, children are taught what to think instead of how to think.

Wow, I guess you would say pretty morbid huh? If you take everything in at once, it can make you depressed. You may feel the chain around your ankle like the elephant. You may resign yourself to stay where you are and accept the condition forced upon you.

Don't give up!

Before you give up or give in. Think about this: Everywhere you look, people like yourself exceed the expectations of the people and circumstances around them. Everyday someone is graduating from college who according to statistics should have died in their first 16 years of life. Everyday someone is doing something spectacular that appears beyond his or her potential. Everyday individuals are exceeding the expectations of others.

These individuals are not listening to the negative voices and are not focusing on their limitations especially those dictated by others. Let me share two short stories about characters that are universal; frogs and peacocks.

Let's start with the frogs. One day in frog kingdom, the frogs decided they would have a contest to see who the best frog was. In their kingdom there was a vast mountain that served as a center - piece for their community. It was decided that the strongest and fastest frogs would compete in contest where they race to the top of this mountain. No one had ever done this before and there were a lot of old frogs who did not believe especially a frog, could do it.

Ten frogs were selected, and the day of the race came. A great crowd came out to watch however many came just to see the frogs fail. They started the race and after 15 minutes on the mountain, 3 of the frogs fell off. The crowd cheered "you can't do it, give up and save yourself." More and more frogs dropped off the mountain each falling by the wayside. The crowd roared, "It's impossible. You can't do it, come back." Finally, they were down to three frogs. While two of frogs struggled, the one in front continued without hesitation completely focused on his task to get to the top. Suddenly the two frogs dropped to the ground. The one frog continued to reach the top. On the top, the frog waved the victory flag and jumped up and down as the crowd roared with amazement. When the frog returned to the kingdom as a victor, the crowd rushed all crying out, "how did you do it?" The frog continued about his business as if they hadn't even spoken. Suddenly, they realized, the winning frog was deaf. He couldn't hear the doubts and negative comments from the crowd. He focused on his inner voice, which encouraged him to his goal.

Morale - The people around you may be what are holding you back. It's not what they say, but what you do that counts. Don't listen to anyone who tells "you can't do something." They may be saying it because they can't do it or because they don't have the courage to try. The second point is something that which may appear to be a limitation may be a strength. **Magnificent individuals** take perceived obstacles and turn them into opportunities.

The Peacock Story

I was told this story by one of my seminar participants. I gave an assignment for the class. They must go out and network for themselves and come back with feedback. One of the trainees stated that while she could advocate for her organization, she could not do so for herself. I told her that was nonsense. She was a representative of her organization. People are more influenced by your presentation and your interpersonal skills than an organization. They teach sales people that they are really selling themselves rather than a product or organization. She responded, "Do you know about the Peacock?" Puzzled, I answered, "Tell me about the Peacock." Well, she said everyone knows that Peacock has beautiful feathers. They are Magnificent! However, what people don't know is that Peacocks have ugly feet. In fact, if a Peacock were to look at the feet, they would run and hide.

I thought for a moment. This is a perfect teaching moment. I responded, "that which you focus on, is what you give power". The peacocks in their wisdom focus their attention on their assets, their wondrous feathers. Their swag is the feathers. They know by emphasizing this gift, they will impress everyone they meet. What they don't do is care about their ugly feet. They don't point to them; bring them up in conversation or allow them to dictate their lives. Many of us can learn from the peacock. Instead of emphasizing what we can't do or what we don't have and let that dictate our lives, we should focus on our gifts and let our assets empower us to move forward. In order to exceed your expectations, you must change how you feel about yourself. You must destroy all those self-imposed boundaries. Someone once defined fear as **False Evidence Appearing Real**. Fear only exists in our minds. It is not an entity on the earth. We create and nurture fear in ourselves. We also nurture fear in others and even our children. We discourage their goals and tell them to be more realistic.

The people who become great disregard the realistic, ignore the circumstances and overcome the obstacles to do the things they want in life. They see beyond the matrix. They create their own reality and live according to their own standards and principles.

The trailblazers and pioneers in our history have always gone where others dared to go. Contrary to popular belief, they started out as ordinary people. As they ventured and took on challenges, they began to do extraordinary things.

The sum of your deeds not only defines our character but establishes your destiny. Do you want to start to exceed your expectations? You can begin by first focusing on your assets. Do a self- assessment.

What are you good at doing? You have been given skills for a reason. Ask yourself, what am I passionate about? You are given passion for a reason. If your passion and skills are connected, you're on the way to becoming greater than you were. Many people fail to connect their passion and their skills.

Once you connect your passion to your skills recognize and give thanks. Acknowledge that you have been provided with extra value in this area. The way you exceed expectations is by giving value to the world. Think of anyone great in the world. They are known not because of what they did for themselves but for what value they provided to the world.

You don't have to take on the world. Start where you live. Start with your family and your community. Use your **Magnificent** Mind you have been given. You have been blessed and it's for a reason.

Your next steps are to set goals. These goals start with you. Refine your skills. As Covey, author of **Seven Habits of Effective People**, states, "Sharpen the Saw". Practice your skills, become the master. Set goals that will take you to the next level. Simultaneously, set goals to utilize your skills in your immediate world. Regardless of your specialty you can share that with the world. You may be a great speaker, rapper, artist or musician. Use your skills to make a difference.

Will Smith born in ghetto streets of West Philadelphia. Will Smith went on to become an Emmy Awarding Rapper and then transformed himself in an Oscar nominated Actor earning millions of dollars per project. Will spoke on the difference between talent and skills. He said that talent is something that you have naturally. Skill is only developed though hours and hours of beating on your craft. He adds, "I never really viewed myself as particularly talented. Where I excel is ridiculous, sickening work ethic. While the other guy is sleeping, I am working. While the other guy is eating, I am working. There is no easy way around it, no matter how talented you are; your talent is going to fail you if you are not skilled. If you don't study, if you don't really work hard and you don't dedicate yourself to being better every single day, you will never be able to communicate with people with your artistry the way you want.

I worked in the entertainment field in the City of Philadelphia; home of Gamble and Huff. Philadelphia International Records and some of the greatest vocalist and groups in the world who have come out of Philly. The city is full of talented individuals; however, few have the skill to make it. Will Smith shared a great point. Talent will take you only so far. It's the process of developing your talent and becoming a skilled artist that will make the difference between success and failure.

Finally, Gandhi said, "Be the change, you want to see in the world". Moreover, to overcome the Matrix you must "See the change you want to be in the world".

BONUS FOR READERS - Want to keep current with the latest ideas, tips and advice on how you can be the best you can? Visit www.theconnectornetwork.com and sign up. You also can Text -

Be Magnificent! Exceed Your Expectations

B-Mag to theConnector@verizon.net for free videos and our social digest subscription.

Chapter 12

7 KEYS TO EFFECTIVE LEADERSHIP

Okay, so you find yourself in a leadership position over a team of individuals. You got a great group of knowledgeable individuals who are used to "doing their own thing" but not working together. The question is how do you pull them together as a group respecting their skills yet directing their efforts?

The success of your team will directly be affected by your own leadership effectiveness. If you want to increase your effectiveness as an individual, you need to increase your leadership skills. James Maxwell, leadership expert states that there is a direct correlation between your effectiveness and your leadership skills. By focusing on developing and refining those attributes possessed by top leaders, your efficacy will grow, and your outcomes will be more apparent.

Here are seven keys you can utilize to open the door to effective leadership.

1. You have a Vision - All effective leaders have a vision. Vision has nothing to do with what is before your eyes but what you see in the future. Effective leaders have an image of a project or workshop completed. They can see what a highly functioning team looks like. They can convey this vision to their team members. When it comes to successful leadership, the more powerful the vision; creates more effective the leader.

2. **You must be motivated.** If you want to inspire others, yourself MUST inspire you. Inspiration means to be" in spirit" meaning that first it's "inside you" and then it's spiritual. In order to inspire others, you must first feel it inside yourself. Inspiring others is like lighting a candle. You must first possess the flame in order to make it work. This means you believe the mission and you believe that your group members can do it. Motivation is like electricity. Where you connect the current is where the energy will flow. But you need to have a source. You are the source.

3. **You know your team** – Talk and connect individually. Each member of your team needs to be considered individually. Everyone has something that is special about him or her. Your job as a leader is to find out what is special about your team member. Find out their passion and validate it. And that will be your key to getting loyalty and respect. The better you know your people, the better you will be able to motivate them.

4. **You present the work in a positive light** – If you are reluctant about the job or assignment, your team will be reluctant as well. If you don't believe, how do you expect your team to believe? Remember you bring the energy whether it is positive or negative. Always frame the mission in positive terms. You may disagree or not understand the goals but the standard of excellence that

your team brings should be the focus. Be honest and realistic but don't be pessimistic.

5.   **You are resourceful** – Provide your team with what they need in order to get the job done. Go out of your way to ensure they have the tools and information necessary to get the job done.

6.   **You establish and monitor lines of communication** – Ensure everyone knows who's taking the lead and to whom they should report. Establish phone trees and lines of communication between the team members. Get people talking and looking out for each other.

7.   **You ensure the team celebrates their success.** Praise and validate good work. Evaluate your outcomes and critique negative outcomes honestly. At the end of each project, event and initiative make sure you give closure with recognition of the good work of the team and the individual contributions of the members. This is vital to the continued success and motivation of your team.

BONUS FOR READERS - Want to keep current with the latest ideas, tips and advice on how you can be the best you can? Visit www.theconnectornetwork.com and sign up.

Be Magnificent! Exceed Your Expectations

Chapter Thirteen

CLOCKING YOUR LIFE: EFFECTIVE TIME MANAGEMENT

One of the challenges in being effective in pursuit of your goals is managing your time. As the saying goes, **"Either you manage your time, or your time will manage you."** This chapter will provide you with some tips in managing your time and managing your life.

1. **Monitor your time** – In order to better manage your time, you should begin by examining how you use your time. Look at the time wasters and things you do to avoid doing what is necessary. There things maybe seen as unpleasant or boring work. Start a journal where you log in where you are spending your time. You can identify time wasted as well as productive time. You will recognize when you are most productive and least productive. Remember procrastination is the enemy.

"Time equals life; therefore, waste your time and waste your life, or master your time and master your life.

Alan Lakein

2. **Make sure you are doing the important stuff.** Eliminate dead-end tasks and refuse to do

unimportant or non-productive tasks. Taking control of your time means you are taking control of your life. You will be surprised at how you spend a lot of your time on unimportant and relevant activities that do not advance your life or your agenda.

"The key is not spending time, but in investing it."

Stephen Covey

3. **Read quickly** - Learn how to skim and speed read, when appropriate. This will add a new dimension to your life. Speed-reading will cut hours off your study time. You will develop the habit of quick comprehension and swift acquisition of knowledge and resources.

"The one thing you can't recycle is wasted time."

Unknown

4. **Decide quickly** - Train yourself to make quick decisions. Avoid delays in decision-making unless you are sure that valuable information is forthcoming. The most effective leaders in business and industry are individuals who can make quick decisions. Many times, when you dwell on a situation, you tend to over analyze. Analysis can lead to paralysis, which leads to lack of action and no outcomes.

"Never leave till tomorrow which you can do today"

Ben Franklin

5. **Plan projects** – Stick to the plan. Since plans have beginnings, objectives, timelines and identification of resources required, having a plan is essential to your individual success. A strategic plan helps you see the target, the direction and the necessary steps needed to achieve them.

"Rather than focusing on what's urgent, learn to focus on what is really important"

Unknown

6. **Set goals and priorities** - Keep focused on your goals and priorities throughout the day.

"He who every morning plans the transaction of the day and follow up on the plan, carries a thread that will guide him through the labyrinth of the busiest life."

Victor Hugo

7. **Concentrate** - The ability to focus and maintain concentration on task is a powerful skill.

"Until we can manage time, we can manage nothing else."

Peter Drucker

8. **Set Deadlines for yourself and others** - Goals without deadlines is like taking a walk without a

destination. You don't know where you're going or when you have arrived.

"Time is the coin of your life. It is the only coin you have, and only you can determine how it will be spent. Be careful lest you let other people spend it for you."

Carl Sandburg

9. **Take a break** - Schedule a break at work. Take a walk. Clear your head. Learn how to mediate for reducing stress and relaxation.

"The bad news is time flies. The good news you're the pilot."

Michael Altshuler

10. **Reward yourself** - Give yourself a reward when completing a task. But don't reward yourself until completion.

"Until you value yourself, you will not value your time. Until you value your time, you will not do anything with it."

M. Scott Peck

11. **Learn to tactfully say "no"** - "Time interrupters" are people who ask for things that take you way from your

goals. Learn how to say no and redirect people who just want to talk.

"Ordinary people think merely of spending time. Great people think of using it."

Author unknown

12. Use a Call back system for telephone calls - One of the best ways to manage your time and utilize phone power is schedule your phone calls both outgoing and incoming. Make phone appointments.

"Nothing is a waste of time, if you use the experience wisely."

Rodin

There you have it twelve incredible tips for managing your time more effectively. Now all you must do is find the time to assimilate these tips into your life habits. The final advice is when you discover innovative techniques immediately adopt and implement them into your lifestyle. The key is "action equals outcome". Time is always a forward pattern of progressive movement; if you can **"clock your time"** you will progressively realize your goals and ambitions.

BONUS FOR READERS - Want to keep current with the latest ideas, tips and advice on how you can be the best you can? Visit www.theconnectornetwork.com and sign up. You also can Text - B-Mag to theConnector@verizon.net for free videos and our social digest subscription.

Chapter Fourteen

12 SECRETS OF EFFECTIVE PROFESSIONALS

Now at this point, you already have your foot in the door. You got the job, things are happening for you and you want them to continue. You are worried about getting stuck. You may be struggling to keep from falling backwards into old habits and into your old comfort zone. Successful professionals know, life begins at the end of the comfort zones. How can you elevate from where you are to the next level?

Here are twelve secrets that all successful professionals know lead to higher achievement.

1. **Seek Balance** - Set goals for all the faucets of your life. Focus on health, wealth and relationships. Balance mental, emotional, financial, personal and family activities.
2. **Happiness -** is not achieved by working all the time or by spending all your time with family and friends. Set balance with goals on each part of your life.

3. **Set Goals** - The successful professional is always setting and adjusting their goals. In order to keep progressing set immediate (30 day) goals, Quarterly (3 month) goals, six-month, 1 year and 2-year goals. (Your overall strategic plan is based upon a 5 - 10-year schedule).

4. **Put yourself on a schedule and stick to it** - This is the single most efficient way to ensure you make progress especially when comes to physical and financial goals.

5. **Think like a chess player** - Life is a game of chess not checkers. This means plan your moves 3 to 4 moves ahead. Have faith in your plans and be ready when opportunity presents itself.

6. **Tap your inner power** - Make it a daily habit to pray, visualize, affirm and meditate. This is how you keep your goals in front of you and fuel your motivation. Spiritual power is supernatural power.

7. **Tap your outward power** (Exercise physically) this not only provides strengthen and endurance but mental well-being.

8. **Create your own tribe** - Develop your mastermind group. Recruit allies and advocates to actively assist you in pursuing your goals

9. **Lead**- being a leader has many moving parts. They include:

  a. **Command the situation** - Analyze, get input and feedback and then develop your plan.

  b. **Decide what YOU want (first)** - Ensure your actions align with your goals. I have many people get involved and help other people achieve their goals; yet make no progress on their own. They expected the OTHER PERSON to figure out what they wanted and give it to them.

c. **Utilize your team (tribe)** includes them in your planning and implementation.

d. **Act with purpose on purpose.** Be intentional; focus on objectives.

e. **Use Momentum** – Be timely. Seize opportunities as they come your way. You can only take advantage of the opportunity of a lifetime during the lifetime of the opportunity.

9. **Create rituals** - Repetitive behaviors systematically develop habits that productively change your life.

10. **Take massive actions** - Now is not the time to hesitate or be shy. Be powerful. Seek amazing results. Create faith.

11. **Let go of bad unhealthy habits and people** - You need to pour out the beer before you fill your glass with champagne. Your associates determine how far you will go in life. If you anchor yourself to people who weigh you down, you will sink. If you hook yourself to people who are soaring, you will fly.

12. **Expand your horizons** - Get out of the city. Take your show on the road. Meet new people and make new friends. The people who truly appreciate you may be just

outside the city limits. Your new job, new partners, next significant other and destiny awaits you. Go for it.

In conclusion, these 12 secrets will take you to places you have never been. The ultimate secret is "Action equals Outcome". You must do them for them to work for you. Remember always exceed your expectations.

BONUS FOR READERS - Want to keep current with the latest ideas, tips and advice on how you can be the best you can? Visit www.theconnectornetwork.com and sign up. You also can Text - B-Mag to theConnector@verizon.net for free videos and our social digest subscription.

Chapter Fifteen

The Five Key ingredients of Success

Okay, you have decided that you are going to be the best at what you do. You are now looking at what you need to focus on and improve upon to take you to the next level.

We will offer five essential elements you must possess in pursuing success in your own personal arena. These five components: fundamental ingredients in creating positive outcomes that every successful professional must utilize in order to move forward. The five are as follows:

1. Attitude

Your attitude is state of mind or mental disposition toward a person, idea, situation or circumstance. Your attitude can be positive or negative. A positive mental attitude will minimize every challenge and reduce every obstacle. A negative mental attitude will magnify every obstacle and enlarge every challenge. Your attitude will take you places your talent would not.

A positive attitude will:

* Make you a source of enthusiasm and energy

* **Increase your sense of self -esteem**

* **Provide tenacity in the face of adversity**

Muhammad Ali had a powerful positive mental attitude. When he was a young boy, bullies confiscated his bike away from him. Ali felt weak and powerless as a result of this encounter. Ali decided to join a gym to learn how to fight. In his lifetime, Ali fought his way to three world heavyweight boxing championships all the while exclaiming he was the greatest boxer of all time.

In the face of losing his boxing license and facing jail time due to his objections to the war in Vietnam. Ali kept his positive attitude and stood up for his beliefs about his religion and culture. Ali gracefully persevered through his challenges to regain his title and become known as the Greatest. Ali also possessed an amazing confidence in his skills and abilities. Attitude and confidence are essential to becoming Magnificent.

2. **Confidence**

Confidence is belief in your abilities and your skills. It is part of something called inner game. Confidence is the ability to feel beautiful without needing someone to tell you. It's the courage to do things, others would not do. Confidence is a mental state that you must project in order to convince your potential employer, partners, mate or business associates that you possess. Lack of confidence is the number one reason people give for rejecting someone. Sometimes if you only have this quality, you can get what you want. The lack of confidence could mean the difference between success and failure. True confidence is not the absence of fear, rather the ability to act in spite of your fear.

3. Plan

You must have a plan. Your plan includes your goal, strategy tactics, and a timeline for achievement. Attempting to move ahead without a plan is like taking a trip without a map. If you don't know where you are going-- you could end up anywhere. Every plan has a ultimate goal, objectives/actions, timeline, identified resources including people; you may need to achieve it.

4. Execution

Execution is another word for performance. You can possess all the above qualities but if your execution is poor, you will never obtain your goal. Great execution comes with visualizing your actions before you take them. Successful executors create a movie in their mind doing exactly what they will do before they do it. They create a successful experience in their minds and then make it reality. Whether you are going to a job interview or trying to meet a new love, what you can conceive and believe, you can achieve.

Gabby Douglas is an Olympic Team Gold medalist because of her superb execution. Gabby, a US Women's Artistic gymnast won gold medals in both the team and individual all-around competitions in the 2012 London Summer Olympics. She is the first woman of color of any nationality and the first African-American gymnast in Olympic history to become the Individual All-Around Champion. Gabby is also the first American gymnast to win gold in both the gymnastic individual all-around and team competitions at the same Olympic games. She understands the value of execution.

5. __Evaluate and Adjust__

Always check your progress. Analyze your moves and the necessary modifications. Always be prepared to adjust your plan. Sometimes the road is different from your map and you may have to adapt to the changes.

When Michael Jordan was in high school, he was cut from the school team. Did he give up on basketball? Of course not! Instead, he analyzed his moves and adjusted. Michael Jordan is a former American basketball player who led the Chicago Bulls to six NBA championships and won the Most Valuable Player Award five times.

These five components are the ingredients for an aspiring professional to utilize in their quest for success.

- Keep a positive mental attitude
- Be Confident
- Plan your work
- Execute superbly
- Evaluate and Adjust methods

Remember always Exceed expectations- Be Magnificent!

BONUS FOR READERS - Want to keep current with the latest ideas, tips and advice on how you can be the best you can? Visit www.theconnectornetwork.com and sign up. You also can Text - B-Mag to theConnector@verizon.net for free videos and our social digest subscription.

Chapter Sixteen

HOW TO LIVE YOUR LIFE WITH PURPOSE ON PURPOSE

Living life with purpose on purpose means that you are living your life with a vision. Make sure your actions are precise and intentional. Living your life this way allows you to focus on what is important and guarantees progress toward what you feel is important.

Have you ever felt like your life was meaningless? You seem to lack direction, energy and motivation. Every day you go to work and there is no satisfaction in what you do. You just go through the motions with no real direction.

MAKE A DECISION

This is because you have not made an important decision about your life. I am not talking about superficial goals like buying a new car or new additions to your wardrobe. This is not about pursuing luxuries and accessories. It's about deciding on what your values are in life. It's about living your life with principles which you stand by. It's about focusing on an overall goal that goes beyond superficiality.

PLANT A SHADE TREE WHERE YOU WILL NEVER SIT

Living life with purpose and on purpose is about seeking an outcome from your actions. It could be about improving the lives of others, changing the environment where you grew up or giving back in time, skills, money and love to a place where you come from. It also could be about planting a shade tree where you will never sit. Deciding you are going to live your life with purpose means sacrificing those meaningless activities for thing that are worthwhile.

FIND YOUR SPIRITUAL PATH

So how do you do it?

First, you go to a spiritual place in your existence. This place will be the fuel for keeping you on track and moving. Finding the "why" for what you do is extremely important. Learning why you are here can be a major turning point in your life. Deciding to pursue your "why" can be a major turning point in your world.

LOOK INSIDE YOUR PASSION

Looking for your purpose - Look inside your passion. Finding your passion can be like discovering the prize in a Cracker Jack box. It could be something that comes easy to you. It also could be something that you said you would never do. For example, your purpose could be to work with at-risk teenagers. This thought may have repulsed you in the past. You thought-the last thing you would do is work with this population. Then you discover that your skills, abilities and knowledge, make you uniquely qualified work with and develop teen-agers.

Many individuals have pursued superficial goals chasing luxuries and what they thought was the finer things in life. They chased these goals without connecting them to values or principles. The ending result was they did things they were ashamed of. Many of them end up in jail. The amazing thing about this is once in jail, they realized their potential and their true purpose. While in jail, they obtained master's degrees and once they reentered the world, become major players behind high causes. There are literally hundreds of individuals who are ex-offenders who are doing major good in the world. This is only because they found their purpose and are now living that purpose.

LIVE IN IT

I know a young man named **Will Little** in South Philadelphia who lived the drug dealer's life and ended up killing someone early in his life. Sentenced to life imprisonment, Little found his purpose and the doors opened up. He was released from prison. He is now influencing the lives of hundreds of young men through his mentoring activities. Little now lives his life with purpose.

BROKEN WINGS

There's a sister named **Natasha Harris**, whose life was all over the place. She was hustling and fighting everyday just to survive. After passing through seventeen foster homes, she was destined to become a statistic. Yet Natasha found her purpose and changed her life. Today, she is CEO of Broken Wings Literacy Center and owner of her own daycare center. She is a book author who teaches young women how to overcome their circumstances. Natasha lives her life passionately and with purpose.

BY ANY MEANS

Malcolm X lived his life as a drug dealer, pimp, thief and hustler. While in prison he found his purpose and become national leader and International legend. Malcolm found his purpose and began living it and his life changed.

Positive outcomes come easier when you are on your path. Not living with purpose is swimming against the waves. After a while you get tired and give up. When living on purpose life's struggles become motivation to do more. You see obstacles as opportunities. You realize that you have the rest of your life to live the best of your life.

Living life on purpose and with purpose creates legacy. It gives meaning to your existence and tells the story of your life. Greatness comes from purpose.

BONUS FOR READERS – Have you signed up at www.michaelricespeaks.com so you can be notified when onl-line courses, workshops, seminars and personal coaching is available? Do it now!

Chapter Seventeen

HOW TO INCREASE YOUR PERSONAL POWER

Let's speak about the greatness that we have inside of us. Many of our skills go untapped. Some people wander through life without even coming close to utilizing their potential. Inside them are songs that are unsung and books unwritten and stories untold.

Les Brown often speaks about how the cemeteries are filled with the unused gifts that people failed to use in their lives. We are going to focus on four powerful gifts you always possess and carry with you . These gifts are like instruments in a toolbox. Tools when used make life a lot easier. Tools unused are like carrying an umbrella during a downpour. You are prepared but not executing. In this chapter, I am going to help you reframe some common things you do into powerful tools at your disposal.

YOUR SMILE

Smile - Your smile is one the greatest gifts that you can offer someone you don't know. One of the definitions Webster provides is that a smile is "the bestowal of a blessing." It is said that people who smile are three times more attractive than people who don't smile. Imagine all the millions of dollars spent on beauty products, when all you had to do was smile. Your smile is an essential tool when meeting new people, interviewing for jobs, selling products and getting the attention of the opposite sex. When you smile, your face says you are friendly and likable. These qualities cultivate trust. Smiling make you more approachable and more likable.

"Always remember to be happy, you never know who is falling in love with your smile."

EYE CONTACT

Eye Contact - Eye contact is essential with meeting someone new because it promotes trust and credibility. It has been said that your eyes are the mirrors to your soul. If you are unable to maintain eye contact when you are talking about yourself, your product or service, you will not come across as trustworthy or believable. Think about this. Your eyes send out vibrations that will bounce off of objects and hits the lens of your eye revealing an image. Vibrations are just another form of energy. In other words, when we look at someone, we are actually sending rays of energy in their direction. Have you ever felt someone watching you? What you are feeling is that energy focused upon you. When you make eye contact you are focusing your energy upon the person you are looking towards. When we look at each other, we are exchanging energy; a visual collaboration. Want to make a connection? Use your eye contact as a first step.

THE HANDSHAKE

Handshake - Your handshake is part of your self-image. A handshake projects your confidence and it is a physical connection. While your handshake should be firm, don't attempt to break the hand of your new contact. Conversely, don't do the "noodle" by offering a limp, weak handshake. This suggests lack of enthusiasm and energy.

Physical contact by humans is as essential as flower needing water. In fact, lack of physical contact with a baby can lead to a condition called, "failure to thrive." As human beings we need human contact to grow and develop. By extending your hand you are initiating and moving the initial contact to the next level.

The handshake is a tradition handed down through centuries and transcends cultures. Originally, handshake was used by rival factions by showing your hand was not baring a weapon; you showed the other person you were safe and trustworthy. Handshakes have many uses. We show gratitude and agreement via handshakes. Many secret societies use handshakes to identify members. We use handshakes upon meeting someone and when we are parting company. When we agree, the handshake seals the deal.

POSITIVE MENTAL ATTITUDE

Positive Mental Attitude (PMA) - Your positive attitude is an expression of your personality. While it is invisible to the eye, it acts as a magnetic force connecting you with your new contact. Having a positive mental attitude is attractive. It demonstrates confidence, generates trust and fuels motivation. PMA supercharges your other tools including your smile, handshake and eye contact. Demonstrating PMA is essential to winning interviews and making strong impressions on management and staff. PMA is essential to overcoming adversity and defusing negative people. Listen to inspiring music to generate positive emotions, which you can share with others.

USE YOUR GIFTS

There was an old cartoon called Felix the cat. It was about a cat that in each episode faced many different challenges. However, when Felix faced a difficult circumstance, he simply reached into his bag and came out with a solution. Your smile, eye contact, handshake, and positive mental attitude are tools you always have with you helping you to make a good impression and influence situations. They are readily available, and you don't need to remember to pack them in your bag. Putting together these powerful tools will make is easier to make new contacts, expand your circle of influence and increase your ability to address adversity. They are inherent powers at your disposal.

BONUS FOR READERS - Want to keep current with the latest ideas, tips and advice on how you can be the best you can? Visit www.theconnectornetwork.com and sign up. You also can Text - B-Mag to theConnector@verizon.net for free videos and our social digest subscription.

Be Magnificent! Exceed Your Expectations

Chapter Eighteen

How to become the Boss everyone loves

RELATIONSHIP BUILDING

Remember your best supervisor? Sort of combination of your favorite teacher combined with your favorite uncle. They listened, had patience and believed in you. They also were willing to stretch the rules every now and then.

What traits did he or she display that endeared them to you? Great leaders always have people who want to do things for them. They make people feel good about themselves, so people want to be around them. I remember my best supervisor had three phrases he used with everyone whenever there was a challenge to be addressed.

1. **"It ain't that deep"** - Regardless of what the issue was, he always kept his composure and said these words.
2. **"It will be alright"** - Keep it positive and see the opportunities in the opposition.

3. **"What they going to do-fire me?"** Bend the
    rules for your people. Leadership is challenging the
    rules that don't make sense or are not productive.

Here are some basic techniques for becoming that loveable
person everyone wants to be around.

1. **Smile** – Make it a habit to smile at your team
    members. When you smile at people, it makes them
    feel good about themselves. Normally, when you smile,
    at someone, they smile back. Smiling releases
    endorphins and they generate a feeling of well-
    being. When you exchange smiles, they attribute their
    good feeling to you. If you look like you're being
    interrupted every time someone comes to your office,
    your staff will avoid you. Always keep a welcoming
    smile.

2. Be Cheerful. – No one wants to hang around a sad sack
or someone who is angry all the time. People seek out
positive people because they make them feel good about
themselves.

3. Act like a person having a lot of fun – you will be
amazed how you will attract people toward you. If you
seem like you love the work and enjoy doing it, your team
will want to join in the fun.

4. Ask your team members about themselves -
Everybody, favorite subject is themselves. By showing
interest, you make them feel like they are interesting. In
fact, one of the sweet sounds in any language is your own

name. When speaking with your team members use their names frequently.

5. Talk about what interests them - Of course, you need to start by finding out what interests them. Utilize their interests and hobbies in coaching them in doing their work.

6. Be empathetic - Listen and feedback. Covey says, "Seek first to understand and then to be understood. Use "you" instead of "I" statements. Instead of saying, I understand how you feel, say so "**you** feel sad, angry, frustrated" or whatever emotion they may be displaying. This approach makes the conversation about them and not about you.

7. Use body language – Reflect their body language when you see them use non-verbal heads nods, eyebrow flashes, smiles and winks. Mirror their body language. They will wonder why you seem to grow on them.

8. Utilize proximity, frequency, duration and intensity - In the "Like Switch" former FBI agent Jack Schafer talks about how he 'turned" foreign agents over time by frequently being physically close to them for long periods of time. Be sure to take time to talk with your team everyday just to see how they are doing. Don't come across like you are checking on them to see if they are working. Rather ask about their day, family and if they need your support on anything. This is called a "check in".

9. Practice good hygiene – No one wants to be around someone with funky underarms or bad breath. If you smoke always keep some mints with you. A nice cologne or perfume or even a lotion that smells good is refreshing if its not overdone. Smelling something good makes a person feel good and they will associate that feeling with you.

10. Go deep - Get your staff to talk about their childhood or growing up. Find out why they choose their profession or what they really want to do. This conversation deepens relationship and gives you a reference and at times explanations for how your staff reacts to different situations. This will bring you closer to them and they will be more willing to work with you or for you.

Don't talk about other teammates behind their back and don't embarrass teammates in front of their peers. However, saying good things about person behind their back will create good feelings. In both instances, you can bet it will get back to the person you will talking about.

Don't emphasize your title to get compliance. This is the lowest level of leadership and your team will unwillingly follow you, however morale and motivation will be low. This will also cause resentment and make you the number topic around the water cooler.

Utilize these tips, you will become a sought-after supervisor or boss. When the conversation comes up about great people to work for, they will be talking about you.

BONUS FOR READERS - Want to keep current with the latest ideas, tips and advice on how you can be the best you can? Visit www.theconnectornetwork.com and sign up. You also can Text - B-Mag to theConnector@verizon.net for free videos and our social digest subscription.

Chapter Nineteen

Final Thoughts

I have some final thoughts to leave with you. The expectation is that some of the words, stories and essays within this book will provide you with insight, inspiration and comfort in dealing with the trials of life. However, the truth of the matter is that we are all going die. You probably won't get to choose how or when, but death is inevitable.

What you do get to choose is how you're going to live. From this moment on you can make decisions on how you going to feel about yourself, your purpose in life and how your going about living your life. Sometimes you don't get to choose what happens in life because stuff happens. You win and you lose. You love and you get your heart broke. Someone you trust will let you down. Someone less qualified than you will gets the job. You'll be on a roll and get a setback.

Life is about seasons. It is guaranteed after summer will come a fall. And even after the coldest winter, spring will arrive. There are no permanent seasons. Just like you got to be prepared for a cold spell when it comes, you got to get ready to shred that protective clothing and enjoy the change in weather when it comes. This is just how life goes.

You must be prepared mentally and emotionally for setbacks.

"The lesson taught at this point by human experience is simply this, that the man who gets up will be helped up; and the man who will not get up will be allowed to stay down. Personal independence is a virtue and it is the soul of which comes the sturdiest manhood. There can be no independence without a large share of self-dependence and this virtue can not be bestowed, it must be developed within."

Frederick Douglas

The reality is, it's not about what happens but how you deal with what happens. You can't allow situations or circumstances to dictate your attitude or your life. Life is more about taking punches than throwing punches. If you can survive the knockout blow, you are winning. Most people don't.

It's like we are in a tug of war. On one side we have love, happiness, goodness, courage, passion and security at the other end we have hate, evil, sadness, fear and anxiety, remorse and danger. We get to choose who's in control and who we want to give our focus and support to. The battle continues our entire life.

I grew up in a community where according to the statistics most of us would be dead by age 24. I saw death, drugs and depression everyday coming up. With no daddy in the home to guide them, their mothers struggling trying to raise their siblings and trying to teach them how to survive many of my friends gave up early in life. We grew up with alcoholics on corners, crack heads in the alley, physical violence within the home while dealing with teen-age pregnancies and youth gang wars. Our parents wouldn't listen, and our teachers didn't care.

Even under these conditions, many of us prospered. It was like the ordeals and challenges were the fuel for overcoming obstacles. While some used the fact, they had no father at home and that our mothers were overwhelmed as excuse to run wild, others used it as motivation to implement a plan to overcome their circumstances and create a positive story.

> **"'The true measure of a man is not how he acts during times of comfort and convenience but how he stands during times of controversy and challenges"**
>
> **Rev. Dr. Martin Luther King, Jr.**

While at same time, my brothers succumbed to the lure of the streets, submitting to the obstructions such as family fragmentation, educational challenges and financial obstacles, others have excelled, overcoming their environment to create a new legacy for themselves and their families.

Success in life is not a destination; it's a journey. It's dealing with life's challenges and being able to keep your head up. Success is finding a reason to smile in the face of adversity. It's dusting your shoulders off, when facing opposition and recognizing you were born to win.

Diamonds are created by applying pressure. Character is determined not how you act when things are going your way, but who you are when times get tough.

You are built for life. God does not put anything in front of you cannot survive. In fact, many of the challenges set before you are tests, to see how much you want them. Sure, it's not easy. Have you ever appreciated something that came easy as much as something you had to work for? You got to choose to take on the challenge. Act or do nothing. Submit or resist, the choice is up to you. Survival is in your DNA.

Many of us are the descendants of the people who would not die. Our blood is the blood of the best. Our ancestors were kings and queens. They created medicine and mathematics. They bought science and structure to the world.

When the colonists came to the motherland and enslaved the captive Africans, they did not choose the weak, helpless, unhealthy or disabled. No, they chose best of the best. The trip from the village to the ship was a laborious journey and many did not survive. Only the strongest and most enduring prevailed from the whips of the oppressors.

The captive cargo endured physical assault and humiliation over the voyage the new world. Chained together stacked like sardines often urinating and defecating on each other; they survived the diseases, rats and torture. Finally arriving at the new world, they would be introduced to an oppressive, demeaning and physically demanding involuntary lifestyle for generations. However, through the bondage, lynching, genocide, bigotry and racism as a people they survived.

Think about that, after being separated from your family, stripped of your religion, denied your culture and your freedom and having to pursue your education and development under an oppressive regime living everyday with the threat of possible death, they survived. They overcame these challenges to become scientists, inventors, doctors, engineers, lawyers and world leaders.

This is the DNA that flows in your veins. It is one of an unconquerable and invincible spirit that cannot be denied. Some of us live up to our potential while others fail to embrace the legacy. What we know is that within us is a power and strength that has been handed down though our ancestors.

One thing we know is that when faced with challenges, adverse circumstances, oppression, discrimination, hatred, bigotry, jealous and evil, is when the real players step up. We know if you get knocked down and can still look up, you can get up. If you can get up, you can win.

Every set back is a set up to a comeback.

One thing I learned in life, there is no such thing as a coincidence. Everything happens for a reason. People, situations and circumstance are set forth in our lives to teach us to grow and reveal our true power.

If you ever overcame an obstacle in your life, then you know. Although sometimes, you forget or choose to ignore the power you been given. You have been bestowed great power. The greatest power is your mind and the ability to manifest everything you desire in life though faith and commitment to your higher power. Don't ignore the miracles you have been experiencing all your life. Remember all those times when you thought you couldn't go on. Remember the pain you thought would never go away. Well, you are here today, ready and able to take on another challenge and win.

Remember, each one of us is here to write our own story. We are the heroes of the story. We are the champions meeting the challenges. Today decide to be the star of your movie. Set your goals, create your legacy and manifest your destiny.

Exceed your expectations – Be Magnificent!

BONUS FOR READERS - Want to keep current with the latest ideas, tips and advice on how you can be the best you can? Visit www.theconnectornetwork.com and sign up. You also can Text - B-Mag to theConnector@verizon.net for free videos and our social digest subscription.

Elements of the Community, Inc

ABOUT THE AUTHOR

Michael Rice aka "The Connector"

Michael Rice has bought thousands of individuals and organizations together to fulfill mutually supportive goals and common missions. He has trained hundreds of individuals in leadership skills, relationship building, project management, strategic·planning and community engagement.

As a leader in his field and industry, Mr. Rice teaches the "Magnificent Manifesto" -Eleven Principles of Effective Leadership. He believes in the advocacy of **"Urban Networking- the development of mutually beneficial relationships.**

As a publisher and author, he reaches thousands of individuals through his weekly "The Connector," an online business & social digest. The Connector offers insight, advice and guidance to Urban Professionals nationally.

Michael Rice has been acclaimed as an Award-Winning Social Innovator, Community Engagement Specialist, PR specialist, Leadership Coach, Trainer and Master Networker. He has been recognized by PA State Legislate and Philadelphia City Council for his work with youth and the community. He has worked with the private and public sectors professionals, trained business, non-profit and community leaders and activists.

Mr. Rice is available for workshops, seminars, keynote presentations and personal coaching for individuals, nonprofits, businesses, public and private organizations. For more information join the Professional Networking Associates at www.theconnectornetwork.com

Email: Theconnector@verizon.net

Author website: www.michaelricespeaks.com

Phone: 215-339-8208

"Live for a Cause; not applause. Live life to express and not to impress and instead of trying to be noticed-make your absence felt".

Made in the USA
San Bernardino, CA
29 May 2020